THE MIRACLE BABY

Israel A. Abimael

Book production by MysticqueRose Publishing Services LLC

ISBN: 979-8-218-61014-2

Acknowledgment

First and foremost, I want to give all the glory to my Lord, Savior, and Redeemer, Jesus Christ. I extend my deepest appreciation to my community, Jesus Christ Ministry Through Love, Deliverance, and Miracles, where I have served as a leader for nearly ten years. You are my rock, and I thank you for praying for me every day.

I would also like to express my heartfelt gratitude to Mr. Paul Rangel, who God brought into my life as my destiny helper. He introduced me to Lynnette Steele, who, in turn, introduced me to her daughter, Porsché Mysticque Steele. I am deeply indebted to Porsché for her patience and understanding of my background, which is French. She took the time to help me write my book, and I was touched by her passion for helping me.

Porsché edited the book, provided valuable advice, and shared tips about writing from the perspective of a CEO. She is the driving force behind the success of this book. Additionally, she hired the book cover designer, Uche Aham-Okehie, and interior designer, Oluwaseun Edunjobi, to whom I am also grateful. Whatever I needed related to writing or publishing, Porsché was there to support me. She is the founder and CEO of MysticqueRose Publishing.

I want to thank my lovely children, who read and provided feedback on the rough draft of the book. I could not have accomplished this without the support of my sisters, Lyna

Edwige Diallo and Marie Viviane Ble, who my mother did not give me. God bless you abundantly, sisters, for showing me love during my hardest times. You have always been there for me, supporting me both financially and spiritually. You shed tears with me during my struggles as a homeless person and offered me your home. I love you both. Thank you!

I also want to honor the memory of my father, Mr. Bessou Laurent, and my mother, Zoua Pauline. They are the reasons God brought me into this world.

To my readers, I want to emphasize that writers exist because of you. My motivation for writing this book is you. I wanted to share my testimony and convey that you are neither an accident nor a coincidence. Regardless of how you were born or what family you come from, you are perfectly and purposefully made by your Creator to serve Jesus Christ. He has gifted you with a unique mission. You are an extraordinary person, created by an almighty God to reign. I hope you learn more about yourself while reading this book, as that is the main purpose of my writing. If you would like to discuss anything from the book with me, please feel free to email me at isarelabimael@pischonstudios.com.

Contents

CHAPTER 1

Attempted Kidnapping

When a woman is pregnant, the child is hers alone, but once she gives birth, the village helps nurture the baby as its own. Sadly, there are always exceptions to this rule. Just as a dog has only one way to sit, some people show a nature that doesn't stray far from that.

It's not a Friday, which means I can sleep in. My parents and I share a single bedroom in our small flat, separated only by a curtain. I wake to the whispers and the light patter of feet moving across the floor.

It's my father, preparing for work. I feel grateful for the reassuring warmth of his presence before he leaves. His face has Asian features, and his tall, athletic build resembles a basketball player's. I usually only see him at dinner, and when he's traveling for work, it's once a month at best.

Outside, the chants of campaign volunteers echo through the streets. For the past two weeks, they've flooded the slums, covering every wall and post with campaign posters. The cacophony of noises drowns out the birds' sweet songs and even the rooster's morning call.

Dad moves through the curtain that divides our living spaces into the living room. Before leaving, he pauses to remind me, in his usual stern voice, not to wander too far from home. My mother, stretching and yawning, joins him on my side of the room. She may not be tall like a baobab tree, but her face has the softness of an angel, perfectly complementing her full figure.

I watch them talk from beneath my blanket. Her face glows, as it always does when she's near him. They're discussing the upcoming campaign that only happens once every five years. I've never been to it before, and I can hardly wait. I know I'll enjoy it, especially since I'm known for my dancing—no part of my body can ever stay still when the music starts. They even have nicknames for me: the Little Dancer, Witch, and Margouillat Lizard with Red Hair.

****

In my neighborhood, children are expected to obey all adults and treat every house as their own. I don't mind this, since the adults adore me, but that adoration comes at a price—the hatred of my peers. On good days, they ignore me, but on bad days, they hurl pebbles at me, punch me in the head, or spit on me. When that happens, I fight back with the same aggression, sending them tumbling with my eyes and forcing me to the ground. But it's not just my peers who treat me this way.

Middle and high school students join in the bullying, taunting me with names that bring tears to my eyes. Their words hurt more than any punch. I feel safe only when adults are around. Without them, I'm always on guard, watching out like a tennis match referee. They mock me for the red color of my hair and the white of my eyes. I didn't choose these colors, and I can't change them, so I learned to live with the insults.

It's another morning. The sun's rays, tinted with red, cast a soft glow on my skin as the air feels heavy. I push the feeling aside, focusing instead on gathering my miniature kitchen utensils for playtime under the coconut trees in the middle of our courtyard.

I'm wearing a tank top, panties, and my new shoes, which make me feel glamorous despite Mama insisting they're only for parties. But since she's not home right now, I indulge. The fine beige sand in the courtyard makes our house the perfect spot for playtime, and I pretend I'm cooking on a beach. Our wooden blue house, with its three blocks of one-bedroom apartments, is a familiar playground. I recreate Mama's dishes using herbs I've picked from the papaya trees.

While my parents are away, the neighbors are responsible for watching me. Mama's best friend and our next-door neighbor, Mr. Kouakou, left the house a few minutes ago with his nephews, but his wife can see me from her kitchen, where she's cooking as well.

As I play, the rhythm of the world around me takes over, and I find myself dancing a few times, unable to resist. When my pretend food is finally ready, I lean over and blow out the imaginary fire beneath my pot.

Suddenly, a ten-ton truck approaches, reversing slowly toward me. The back is covered by a black plastic material stretched over iron rods. I ignore it at first, but then the sound of footsteps makes me look up. I see a dark-complexioned man, as tall as my father, leering at me. My heart drops, the hair on my scalp prickles, and a weight presses down on my chest. I stiffen as my eyes darken. Trying to stay calm, I look away and focus on my pretend meal, trusting that the adults nearby will protect me. The truck comes to a stop.

A second man steps out of the vehicle, dressed in a weathered black coat jacket that makes him look like he belongs to a biker gang, with military boots completing the look. Before I can react, his right hand grabs my neck, and his left lifts me off the ground. I struggle, kicking my legs until one of my shoes falls off. I scream with everything in me, but the roar of the truck's engine drowns out my cries. His footsteps are swift, barely touching the ground as he carries me. I pound my fists against his chest, but it's no use. Amid the chaos, I catch a glimpse of Mrs. Kouakou just before I'm tossed into the back of the truck.

As the man jumps back into the vehicle, I hear shouting and see people running toward us—Mama's voice among them. She grabs the first man by the collar, making him sway like a tree in the wind. Someone else rushes to pull me from the truck. Both men tremble as the one inside sticks his head out of the window, frantically gesturing for his partner to hurry. As they try to drive off, my neighbors block their path, and the driver grows agitated as my mama and the others surround the truck, a ball of fiery anger, demanding answers. There's no distinction between who is asking the questions and who is answering them.

The truck is surrounded, and the man inside is forced to respond to the crowd. Finally, Mrs. Kouakou emerges from her kitchen, screaming and waving her arms. Her outburst is met with contemptuous glares. When questioned, the two men claim, "We were just having fun." My mama doesn't buy it. Her hands tighten around the man's collar, refusing to let go. He tries to shake her off, but she clings to him like a bee to honey.

Tears blur my vision as I cling to my mama's leg with all my might. The man is finally pried from her grasp by the neighbors. Both men leap into the truck and speed out of the neighborhood, with the neighbors giving chase but unable to catch them. Mama glares at Mrs. Kouakou without uttering a word.

"I didn't know! I didn't see anything, and I didn't hear the child scream," she pleads defensively.

My body trembles at the scene. The neighbors advise my mama not to leave me under her supervision again, and they suggest she stop letting me sit by the roadside every Friday in a white dress with two plates in front of me. I glance at the others beyond the papaya trees as they murmur amongst themselves. Mama grabs my hand, and we walk back to our apartment, leaving her purse behind. Once inside, she hugs me tightly to her chest, and a soft melody flows from her lips to my ears in her native language as our tears soak her clothes.

"I'm sorry, Mama! I shouldn't have!"

My eyes are squeezed shut as I bury my head in her chest, my words muffled by sobs.

"Forgive me."

It breaks my heart to see her so upset.

"I'll follow you to the market next time, I promise."

Her tears flow silently, trailing down her neck and dampening my hair. She pays no attention to the neighbors' calls. After a while, she bathes me behind the kitchen, using a large iron plate as a makeshift bathtub. Once I'm clean, I have dinner and then crawl into bed, exhausted.

First Day of School

I feel a soft palm on my feet—it's Mommy. I stretch like a puppy in the sand. My eyes flutter open, and through the bedroom window, I see Mother Luminary, beautiful, round, and pale, and her twinkling children in the night sky, watching me.

"Wake up, Genifere! It's time to shower," Mama says.

"Already?" I groan, not wanting to be awake as the sun has yet to rise.

She narrows her eyes but smiles. "Don't be like that. Your hair is like flames."

Minutes later, my feet touch the floor, and I wave my hands tiredly at the ceiling like a sleepy baby. Before she has to repeat herself, I'm in the bathroom. Today is a big day. Mama dresses me in a knee-length, short-sleeved cotton dress patterned with tiny blue and white squares. It feels weird on me.

"I'm proud of you," she says, kissing my forehead and handing me a brown paper-wrapped bread and omelet sandwich.

Her sweetness irritates me, but it also makes me feel like the queen she calls me.

In less than five minutes, she urges me out the door. I feel nervous tremors in my feet like thunder rumbling in the sky. I look up at the sky and spot a helicopter. Mother Luminary and her children, who had been watching us from afar, disappear as we near our destination, replaced by the reddish-yellow hues of the rising sun.

We trade the hard, black road for one scattered with small red gravel. Teenagers in casual clothes pass us, heading toward a tall building enclosed by a metal blade fence—École des Beaux-Arts, the prestigious art school in Ivory Coast.

On our right, there are wild trees, and far ahead, the vast blue ocean seems to meet the infinite sky. In front of us is a courtyard with food vendors and a water fountain in the corner. The teachers' quarters stand about twenty feet from the fountain, followed by five classrooms for elementary students. Beyond the restrooms and another fountain, more classroom blocks continue.

To the left are the sixth-grade classrooms, and next to them, an old building for the fifth graders. Further down is a handball court, and off to the right is a soccer field. All of this is laid out on an oval-shaped plot of land.

There are two towering mango trees with roots sticking out of the ground, reaching as high as my waist. These trees are taller than any other buildings or trees around. The younger kids, in first and second grade, run and play among the roots. Among the children, there's a group of beings that look like Smurfs, but instead of being blue, they are black. Their hair is so long it touches the sand, and their children rest on their backs. My face lights up when I see them. I try to gently pull my hand from Mama's, but she holds on tightly. I want to be with them, to be like them—but the school principal's arrival interrupts my thoughts.

My hair and eyes have turned a bright yellow, glowing like the sun. Mama purses her lips and says, "Stop it! He's your father's friend."

As she and the principal exchange greetings, I can't help but keep my eyes on the peculiar creatures. Their heads are like watermelons perched atop bodies as thin as French bread. Their hands and feet curve like parentheses, which they use to cradle their babies and move gracefully.

The principal tries to speak to me, but I'm lost in thought, focused on the creatures. Mama catches my gaze, her expression a silent warning.

"Don't worry, I'll take care of her," the principal reassures her.

I grab Mama's leg and hug it tightly. From where I stand, I have a full view of the playground. I admire the Smurf-like beings as I watch the other children dart around them, chattering and jumping. The creatures seem oblivious, but their presence stirs something deep inside me.

The massive trees don't hinder their movements. My new friends have eyes as large as tangerines, dark and captivating like the midnight sky. Their bellies resemble medium-sized soup pots, and their noses are shaped like little camping tents. I notice the other students, who had been sluggish earlier, are now fighting and throwing stones at each other. It's as if the beings' presence has stirred chaos.

Mama is ready to leave. Her kiss on my forehead lingers longer than usual as she says, "If anyone bothers you, go to the principal." Her face softens, and tears pool in her eyes. "He teaches the sixth graders," she adds before turning to go. As she walks away, I feel the atmosphere shift, and loneliness creeps over me. I keep my eyes fixed on her until she disappears into the crowd of students.

After a while, I make my way toward the Smurf-like beings and lean against the tree roots. Suddenly, a girl's voice echoes near the first building, catching everyone's attention.

She points at the trees and screams, "Over there! Over there! I see them! With their children, huge heads, long breasts, and long hair!"

Chaos erupts. The teachers rush toward her, and the students by the trees flee in all directions. The whole school descends into turmoil. Some kids hide, whispering and pointing at me. I can't hear what they're saying, and I couldn't care less.

The girl, Lucy, lies motionless on the ground, like a deflated tire. Her eyes are closed, but her finger remains pointing toward me. I look away and focus on the roots beneath my feet.

Why did Mama leave me here? The question circles in my mind like a broken record, my thoughts wandering back home and the quiet peace of being undisturbed.

Amidst the uproar, I stay calm, watching as the Smurf-like beings leave, their feet never touching the ground. Meanwhile, Lucy writhes on the sand, her body covered in it.

Students and teachers glance my way, splitting into two groups—one gathering around me, the other surrounding Lucy. Some parents, still lingering in the courtyard, witness the scene unfold. Two teachers try to help Lucy, but she keeps screaming, her voice piercing the air. Eventually, the principal retreats to his office to call her parents.

As the teachers tend to Lucy, punches rain down on my head, accompanied by mocking laughter. It's the third and fourth graders. They assume I'm the one scaring Lucy, and because I remain unfazed, they feel emboldened.

One of them steps right in front of my face and warns, "You insult me, and I'll beat you up."

Others yank at my hair, asking, "What is this?" while the kinder ones shoot me sympathetic glances. One of the kids digs into my backpack, pulling out my cold breakfast sandwich and taking my lunch money.

As anger simmers inside me, my hair turns a deeper red, and my eye color shifts to a dark brown. The change sends my attackers scrambling in fear. But I remain frozen, unable to move as I watch them scatter.

"Talk!" a voice demands from the group. "Alien! She's an alien!" someone shouts.

I drop to my knees, pressing my forehead into the sand. My elbows dig into the ground as I cover my ears with both hands.

"She's a witch! Witch! Witch!" they chant, their voices growing louder and more insistent. I squeeze my eyes shut, trying to block out the noise.

The chaos around me blurs. I wonder where the teachers are, where anyone is to stop them.

Suddenly, the sharp wail of the school siren cuts through the shouts, signaling the start of the school day. The sound scatters the kids like startled birds, but their words still echo in my ears.

"Thank you so much for your support!" shouts a man by the flagpole, addressing the parents lingering in the courtyard. Then, to us, he commands, "Line up by gender!"

The crowd of students organizes into shaky rows, and I'm swept up in the routine. My feet drag as I follow the other first graders into the classroom, trying to make myself invisible. But the stares burn into my back as we file inside.

I'm seated at the third table in the second row, but the torment isn't over. My head snaps back as pain flares in my scalp. I turn, catching sneers on the faces of my new classmates. My seatmate pinches me, and I flinch, but he pulls back when I meet his eyes.

The day drags on. Every moment is filled with tension, whispers, and the occasional jab from one of my classmates. My body aches from the constant strain, and I count the seconds until the final siren sounds, finally releasing me from this nightmare.

"Thank you, children. Read your books, and I'll see you tomorrow," the teacher says as we gather our things.

Mama told me to go home with a big sister from our neighborhood, but I don't know how to find her without drawing attention. I stall, pretending to pack my things slowly, hoping to avoid another encounter. The teacher notices.

"You don't want to go home? It's over! Go on, now!" he urges.

Yeah, right.

I step out of the classroom, my heart pounding, expecting more taunts. But then I see her.

"Mamaaaaaa!" I scream, my voice cracking with joy.

"I missed you, queen!" she exclaims, smiling wide. "I decided to come pick you up so we can walk home together."

Her words feel like a soothing balm to my soul, instantly calming my frayed nerves. I grab her hand tightly, not wanting to let go.

A Second Abduction

My relationship with the other students is like oil and water, especially with Lucy around. I stay out of her sight to avoid her wrath when she spots the Smurf-like beings. Every morning, her parents meet with the principal and our teacher, but despite their concerned faces and constant conversations, nothing changes. Lucy arrives later, dragging her bag and looking defeated. She's often called out of class to gather her things and move elsewhere.

It's the Saturday of my third week—a half-day. The sunlight feels different somehow, casting a strange glow over everything. Today, I feel no fear of the other students; instead, a peculiar unease simmers beneath my skin. I can't explain it, but it stirs my soul in an unsettling way. I stand near the tree in front of my classroom, close to the teacher, as the hot wind presses against me.

There's a war raging inside me, like water boiling over. When the final siren sounds, the whole class erupts in shouts. I don't even wait for the teacher to say goodbye—I dart out of the classroom, leaving faint footprints in the sand as I make my way toward the red gravel area. As I walk, the sounds of the schoolyard fade, and I'm surrounded by silence as if I've crossed into a different world.

Overhead, a flock of pigeons forms a tight circle, almost like a crown above my head. With each step, a deep anxiety grows within me. The road markers sway along with the trees lining both sides of the road, urging me to quicken my pace. I'm nearly at the edge of the black asphalt road, my mind racing. I just want to leave, not waiting for Mama or anyone else.

But just as I'm about to cross, a sleek, French car pulls up and parks in front of me. A wiry man steps out, clutching an empty brown rice bag, and moves toward me with hurried steps. My stomach drops as my mind screams that something is wrong.

Before I can fully understand what's happening, I'm scooped up and stuffed into the bag. My voice bursts out in a scream as he tosses me into the trunk like a sack of rice. The tires roar as the car speeds away, drowning out the sounds of my cries. Inside the trunk, the heavy smell of smoke fills my lungs, different from the kind my dad smokes. This smoke cuts my breath short and makes my head spin. My chest pounds and I feel the urgent need to poke my head out of the bag.

Despite the jolting of the car, I manage to open the bag's flap just as the car stops. I hear footsteps approaching, and then a black man opens the trunk and looks at me. He's different from the wiry man and gives me a strange smile before gently lifting me out. "I love your hair," he says, running his hand through it, then takes my hand and begins leading me down a narrow path.

The trail is flanked by small trees and herbs that sway with the breeze, and the ground bears fresh tire marks. As we walk, I notice the men around us—they're all coated in sweat and mud, their clothes thick and layered like they're ready for snow. Their red eyes shine as if slick with oil, and the scent of rotten fish hangs in the air. One of them, the lookout, paces restlessly, scanning the surroundings with sharp eyes. Towering trees encircle us, and the sun struggles to pierce through their canopy. Strange animal noises echo around, adding to the eerie atmosphere.

As I take in the scene, my chest tightens with dread, but an odd calm also settles over me. Suddenly, a loud whistle pierces the air, and a tall, muscular man with dreadlocks steps out from behind a tree, holding the hand of a girl. She's mixed-race, her hair long, and she wears a school uniform similar to mine, but with a delicate white lace collar. Her face is red, her cheeks wet with tears as she cries for help. Despite the tension in the air, I hold my ground, watching them all with a strange confidence.

The wiry man yells at the girl, who flinches but still holds her ground, meeting his gaze with defiance. The man holding my hand releases me and steps forward, coaxing the girl with false kindness. "Don't scream! We'll give you candies and cookies if you're good. We won't hurt you," he says, glancing back at me with an unsettling smile.

I feel my hair darken, turning brown like dried blood, and my eyes shift to a deep forest floor shade. My insides churn as my heart thuds heavily in my chest, yet there's a strange numbness in my mind. Suddenly, everything blurs, and I find myself detached, watching from afar, as if inside a tall white box. As if I'm standing next to her, I can see Mama gesturing frantically to the teachers and students in a panic, forgetting her grocery basket is still in front of the classroom.

How do I let her know where I am?

I wonder how to signal my location. When I regain awareness, I'm back in the car with the girl beside me, but the man who brought her is gone. Two others sit on either side of us, guarding the doors. As the car weaves through the forest, she thrashes beside me, her thin arms flailing wildly. Though she's small, she pummels the doors and windows relentlessly, her high-pitched cries piercing the air, and I can't escape her punches either. The men speak in hushed tones while the girl continues to sob, her face streaked with tears. The driver eventually snaps at her, "Put your bottom on the seat and don't move!"

Cold, uncomfortable, and needing to use the restroom, I stay silent, too afraid to ask. As we approach the lights of the city, the girl's head droops onto my shoulder, exhausted. I look out the window and see familiar faces in my neighborhood. Do they see me? Should I shout for help? The men's quiet conversation fills the car, and I realize I can understand what they're saying. We pass by the botanical garden, then the cocoa trees behind the psychiatric hospital. Their overwhelming scent makes breathing difficult.

The car jolts over potholes as we approach dense trees and narrow paths. We reach a barricade of branches, and the man beside me steps out to clear them, allowing the car to pass. Once we're through, he replaces the branches behind us. The road is jagged and uneven, tossing us like water in a shaken bucket. Eventually, we come to a stop. The man next to me takes my hand, and the other carries the girl on his shoulder. They light torches, illuminating our way, and the driver leads a few steps ahead. We move for what feels like ten minutes, carefully stepping around tree trunks and bushes until we reach a small clearing shaped like an oval. At its center stands an altar with a cement seat, surrounded by wooden statues, machetes, and other unfamiliar objects.

They extinguish the torches and make me sit on the cement bench beside the girl, who stirs but remains silent. The men step back a few paces, murmuring to each other in a language I don't understand. Suddenly, a shaft of light shines down from above, casting an ethereal glow around me. I sense a presence in the dry leaves behind me, and my hair begins to glow while my eyes turn crystalline brown. My skin prickles as every pore opens, and my hair and body are taut with energy.

"Are you Mr. Bessou's daughter?" a voice asks.

"Yes, uncle," I reply, recognizing the figure that's appeared in the light, though I didn't know him.

"What are you doing here?"

"These men brought me here," I respond.

He turns to the others, shouting, "Hey, you!" They scatter instantly, disappearing into the trees. Taking my hand, he leads me away, and as we walk a few steps, we suddenly appear on the main street near my neighborhood. The city feels deserted, almost like a ghost town. We take a few more steps, and soon, we're standing in front of my mom's cousin's house.

"You're home now, don't be afraid," he says gently.

Looking up, I see a figure approaching us—a woman with bushy hair, wearing a loincloth that falls to her knees and a crumpled camisole threaded with gold. It's Aunt Suzane. The moment she spots me, she clutches her chest, eyes wide with shock. The man calls out to reassure her.

"The little girl you're looking for isn't dead; she's here. It is about 3 am. Please, don't be angry with her," he explains. Aunt Suzane rushes toward me, and I confirm it's me, nodding as she embraces me tightly, peppering my forehead with kisses. She inspects me from head to toe, relief washing over her. "Thank you so much, sir. Wait here with her while I go inform her mother," she says, hurrying off.

As soon as Aunt Suzane leaves, the man tells me, "You're home now." He gestures for me to stay and then vanishes into the night. Minutes later, a crowd gathers, neighbors reaching out to touch me, their cries and shouts blending in a cacophony of relief. They lift me and carry me to my mother, who's barefoot and disheveled, her face streaked with worry. Our yard overflows with people, many in traditional loincloths, some murmuring with shock. My mother clings to me, singing softly in her language, her body trembling as she holds me close. Tears soak my face and hair.

Beings I don't recognize move through the crowd. Aunt Suzane suddenly recalls the man and rushes off with others to search for him, hoping to thank him. They return empty-handed, and questions rain down on me from everyone around. My hair and eyes shift colors as I cling to my mother, who finally takes me inside, shielding me from the noise. Relief replaces the tension, and the crowd's voices soften as a cooking party begins.

The next day, a neighbor brings over a newspaper with a grim headline: "Obscure Cults to the Ancestral Gods Multiply Victims." The front page shows the image of a girl's headless body. Later that evening, my father returns from his trip with the same newspaper in hand. Our yard fills again with neighbors discussing the article's disturbing details. The following day, my father announces, "We should move."

CHAPTER 2

Inner Awakening

I'm in third grade. My new teacher has assigned some of us to a group for studying advanced two-digit math, and thanks to my dad, I'm very good at it. The teacher names me the group leader, and we meet at my house after school. Now, my classmates take turns carrying my backpack to and from school every day. My mama advises me to appreciate their help like a queen would, so I share my breakfast and lunch money with them, as well as with others at school.

Our new neighbors give me odd looks, but I love our new house. It's detached, with a well and mango trees in the courtyard, and its cool clay walls shield us from the heat. A neighbor offers me a white puppy as a welcome gift, and there's always water when I want it, unlike our last apartment. After our fifth group meeting, which ends around 9 p.m., my dad asks me to walk my classmates home. When I return, I arrange my school supplies on the table, but as I do, I sense a brief presence that vanishes as quickly as it appeared. My mama rushes over, asking if I'm okay like she always does when my complexion changes.

In the middle of the night, I'm jolted by a bright light, even with my eyes closed. When I open them, I hear my parents' snores and quiet footsteps nearby. My bones feel like jelly, my limbs refuse to respond, and I feel like a puppet without strings. The ground beneath me trembles, and the curtain separating my bed from my parents' ripples like waves in the sea. My hair stands on end, my stomach feels like a fireball, and as I look around, I see my hair has turned gold, my eyes light brown. Bright light floods the room, though my parents keep snoring loudly. Somehow, I'm both standing at the end of the bed and lying down in my red pajamas. I study my body carefully, memorizing every detail of its position.

My parents' bed is in the way, but that doesn't stop me. In a blink, I find myself amidst towering stones, each dwarfing the skyscrapers of New York. There are no lights in the sky; the stones stand closely together like trees in a dark forest. My clothes have changed to raw leather, and I hide behind a colossal stone, watching strange creatures moving around their camp like military guards. They're as tall as electric poles, and their bodies emit a glow, making them look like enormous brown gemstones. With limbs longer than their torsos and heads bigger than their bodies, they move effortlessly without using their limbs. Each stone imprisons a human.

A sense of urgency grips me, and I realize I'm here to rescue one particular human. We communicate without words—he asks if I'm here to free him, and as I approach his cell, I touch its stone gate, which crumbles like sand. I grasp his hand and pull him out. As we flee, others in nearby cells beg for my help, but time is short. Suddenly, I'm back in my room, my parents still snoring, oblivious to all that's happened.

My physical body hasn't moved, and I slip back into it without trouble.

In the morning, Mama scolds me for waking up late, as it makes her late for the market—she doesn't like leaving before I go to school. She makes my sandwich, and I set off, cutting through a cocoa plantation to get there. It's tough to walk without getting tangled in the herbaceous plants that snare my ankles, tripping me. Every time I walk this path, I hear my name, though there's never anyone around. Finally, I break free and rush to the school courtyard.

But my relief is brief as my bullies approach, hurling insults: "Red hair! Alien! Witch! Adopted!"

My eyes and hair shift colors as they taunt me, and they throw crumpled paper, chalk, pencils, and anything they can find. Among them stands the principal's son, a sixth grader who towers over me. Striking a pose like a character from a Jackie Chan movie, he suddenly kicks me in the back. Reacting instinctively, I grab his shirt, twist him around, and, climbing onto a table, hold his collar, spinning him in circles before flinging him to the ground. I claw at his skin, leaving bloodstains on his shirt and the bench. The same students who taunted me now cheer, urging me on, but I'm only stopped when teachers rush over. Their alarmed faces make it clear they see me as the monster.

As they pull me off him, I cling tightly, my hands still around his neck. The principal arrives, and they take his son to the hospital. At noon, I return to my classroom, but everyone avoids me, watching from a distance. During recess, I go to the food court with my sandwich and lunch money.

One of my tormentors is nearly in tears, watching others enjoy their donuts, so I offer him 100 CFA Francs, our local currency. Other children gather around, eagerly taking the money.

When I return to class, my teacher approaches me, saying, "Genifere, you share so freely with others. You'll be very rich someday because you give even to those who hurt you."

Later, the principal calls me to his office. As I kneel before him, the sun sets, and Mother Luminary and her mysterious lights appear in the sky.

After I've served my punishment, I walk home. I'm not alone—my friend, a towering figure with a foot so large I can't see past it, walks with me. I don't ask who he is, but I can hear his two footsteps even though I only see one foot.

At home, I explain the day's events to my dad, who has just returned from his trip.

The next day, my father storms into the schoolyard, striding toward the principal's office with purpose. Chaos erupts as teachers rush over to see him dragging the principal by his shirt across the cement steps. Blood stains the man's face, his shirt in tatters. When one teacher tries to intervene, my father's fist stops him, so the others only plead with him to stop. Finally, my aunt, also a teacher, intervenes and ushers my father away. Behind them, the principal throws my admission papers on the ground. Some gather them as he's led to the hospital.

My mama hears of the situation and rushes to school, pleading for me to stay enrolled. After some hours, they relent. Back in class, I scribble "palaver" on a scrap of notebook paper and toss it at someone behind me, relishing the laughter from my classmates. When the teacher asks what's funny, no one answers.

After school, I hit and undress one of the bullies, enjoying the thrill of the day before. Now, some students voluntarily carry my school bag home, and I'm crowned the best dancer after winning city-wide dance contests. I defend my friends from bullies and sometimes walk with my towering friend to class. My mama doesn't like to see me fight, but my dad encourages it. I may display strength, but still have assailants, taunting me on the way home with songs and threats.

At home, Mama notices my distress. "What's the matter?" she asks.

"Why am I different?" I respond, then, more hesitantly, "Am I adopted?"

Sadness fills her eyes, and she whispers, "No," her voice thick with emotion.

Her Hidden Origins

My dad gathers us in the first room of the house, sitting on the bed with his legs dangling just above the floor. I sit on a mat in front of him, our eyes locked, while my mama sits to my left. My heart flutters, just as it did when I sat under the old oak tree, eagerly awaiting my first moonlight tale.

Breaking the silence, my dad begins, "Genifere, you're growing up now. It's time you know who your father is." He grips the edge of the bed, his voice steady. "You're in third grade. I think you're old enough to remember many stories."

His breathing quickens, but he presses on: "When I was a young boy, my father was exiled from his village for taking my mother, who was supposed to marry his father. They fled together, only to return after his father's passing…"

He inhales deeply, then begins the tale with a heavy exhale.

"One strange day, the rooster crowed through the village at midday. No one was there to hear it except a few sick women, some pregnant, and me—a five-year-old who had wandered away from the playground to find my mother. I found her in the kitchen, where a clay pot of sauce was simmering over the fire."

My dad's eyes grow moist.

"She lay by the fire, saliva at the corner of her mouth. I reached for her breast and put it in my mouth, enjoyed the sweet milk, then wandered back to my games after a while."

He starts rocking gently as he continues.

"Soon after, a woman screamed from the same kitchen, rushing toward the chief's house, hands clutched to her head. Dust rose in her wake as she cried out, her voice carrying to the far end of the village. People came out, faces twisted in grief. The talking tam-tam sounded, summoning everyone. After an investigation, it was discovered that her rivals—my father's other wives—had poisoned her palm wine with crocodile bile. Though she wasn't from the village, she was beloved, the mother of my father's first son. My father was left to raise me alone, and we grew close. But my father's other wives looked on me with the same disdain they'd had for my mother. Years passed, yet their intentions remained the same."

"When I turned eight, having survived multiple attempts against me, one of the wives approached me. 'My son, come. I left my money in your father's second room. Go get it.' Trusting her, I went in. Just then, she shouted to the family, 'Come quick! He's in the juju room!' My father arrived, and seeing me in that sacred space, his gaze was seething with anger."

A dog barks outside, and I turn my head to look. My dad pauses.

"Are you listening to me?" he asks.

"Yes!" I reply, refocusing as he resumes his story.

"As I tried to explain myself, saying, 'No, you sent me,' my voice was drowned out by the commotion. My father chased me out of the room and exiled me from the village. The room was sacred and closed to everyone because it was reserved for the gods of our family.

"Left on my own, I found myself in the forest, surrounded by animals. The villagers dared not bring me food, as my father was deeply revered, and so I kept my distance from both the village and its people. I spent my nights under the forest canopy, growing accustomed to the company of creatures there. An old man named Tappah, who lived on the edge of the village, would leave his kitchen door open for me, and I would slip in at night to find food, often joined by the animals. One night, as I rested against the trunk of a tree, I felt a powerful force enter me. I was transformed

31

into a giant, with strength beyond anything I'd known. I gained the power to fly and to change shape into any animal. With these abilities, I resolved to confront my father. I was twelve years old."

"But when I finally faced him, I lost. Defeated, I left the forest and made my way to a nearby town, where I enrolled in school. To pay my tuition, I became a wrestler-for-hire, competing in inter-village competitions. After completing my studies, I moved to the capital and took up masonry. My skills were soon in high demand, and I built a reputation as the best in the field. A few years later, I met a man who would introduce me to the woman who changed my life."

My mama interrupts, her voice distant, her elbows resting on her knees as my dad lowers his head. I watch them both closely.

She begins, "I lost my mother when I was young, and a few years later, my father passed away unexpectedly. My uncle Diddy took me in and enrolled me in school when I was thirteen. I remember the excitement of my first day—it felt like stepping into a new world, and meeting people of different backgrounds. They gave us candies and small gifts to make us feel welcome. We students were thrilled, running around the open yard where we'd soon be learning.

"But after just a few hours of class, my uncle and some other parents approached the teacher, asking for the girls to leave and join the kitchen, which led to a disagreement. That was my last day. Afterward, my uncle sent me to live with my eldest cousin, who had just married. I moved to her husband's village, and three years later, I was married too. I became pregnant soon after and was so happy."

A soft smile touches her lips as she reminisces, but my dad gives her a stern look, disliking how she recalls being forced to drop out of school—a loss she often laments, imagining the life she might have led if given the chance.

She continues, "When I was six months pregnant, my in-laws came to me and said, 'The palm tree has borne red seeds.' I felt the baby move and thought it was a blessing. But the child passed away when he was just five years old. During my second pregnancy, they came with another message: 'The trap has caught a big rat.' This child also died, soon after coming home from school. With my third pregnancy, they said, 'There is darkness in the heavens.' That child passed away in his sleep. For the fourth, they came saying, 'The hen overcame the eagle,' and the child also passed."

Her expression hardens as she recounts each loss.

"They continued to bring messages with each pregnancy. With the fifth, they said, 'There is fire on the mountain.' During the sixth, they said, 'The trap caught two bush meats.' For the seventh, they came in the early morning, saying, 'The lion reclaimed the lioness.' And during the eighth, they warned, 'The eclipse is at the point.' The ninth time, they said, 'The rare fish is out of the sea.' One after another, my sons died.

"In the end, I returned to my uncle in Abidjan. My cousin, tired of seeing me in sorrow, introduced me to his friend—Laurent, your father. We married, but I was terrified of having children and did everything I could to prevent it.

Then one evening, as the shadows stretched across the ground, I saw a brilliant light, and in it, a figure of a man walked toward me. I couldn't see his face, and it seemed as though the sea was beneath his feet. His presence was overwhelming.

"'Who are you?' I asked.

"He replied, 'You called me. That's why I'm here.'

"I answered, 'I don't know you. How did I call you?'

"'You called "LAGO." That is what you call the God of Abraham, Isaac, and Jacob! My name is Jesus Christ. I am God. I am here to give you a child who will end your tears. But this child will serve me! Open your hand and approach.'

"I felt my body tremble, my eyes shut tight. 'Just stretch out your hand and take the child,' he said. I reached out, and a surge of energy jolted through me, leaving me shaken. That same month, I became pregnant.

"While I was carrying you, your father was outside, playing checkers with his friend near the kitchen where I was cooking. Suddenly, two snakes appeared. He quickly grabbed a furrow and killed one of them, though his friend protested.

"'Your wife is pregnant!' his friend said. 'You don't know what will happen—you can't take such risks!' On February 10, I gave birth to twins. Just like the two snakes, one died, and you, Genifere, survived."

Revealing Dad's Spirit

It's evening, and Mother Luminaire and her children take over the skies. The earth growls beneath me, and my whole body feels like it's coming apart. My spirit slips away once again, unnoticed by my mama and dad, who remain unmoved in their sleep. This time, I find myself in a radiant city of grand houses, alive with bright lights and bustling streets.

Wide avenues stretch before me, lined with tall palms along narrow borders. I particularly love standing in front of the Hollywood sign—though I don't know its meaning, something about it feels familiar. I'm dressed in a linen dress, white shoes, and a golden crown, walking above the streets filled with people from all backgrounds. As I glide over the crowd, the sleekest cars move like graceful serpents beneath me. Dogs bark and pull against their leashes, sensing my presence even if the people cannot. I hold each dog's gaze, quieting them with just my aura. It's so beautiful here, I wish I could stay. But, as always, I am pulled back.

When I return, my body is different—shifted as if someone else has moved it. Re-entering, I feel a suffocating pressure; my brain stalls, and my hair and eyes flash with new colors before settling. There's a strange presence in the room, an energy I don't recognize, but I'm too exhausted to question it. I let myself drift back to sleep.

At dawn, I sit near the well. My father's shadow stretches over me, blocking the morning light. "You saw a spirit last night?" he asks. I nod, surprised he knows. Squatting close, he whispers in my ear, "It's your mother." An inner voice reprimands his words, piercing my thoughts. As he walks to the kitchen nearby, my mind reels. *How did he know what I saw?*

That day, he doesn't give me any money as he usually does. On my way to school, passing by the cocoa trees, my one-footed friend appears and calls out, "Check by the big tree—you'll find something." I hurry to the spot, brushing away some leaves to reveal a 500 CFA note, just the amount my dad typically gives me. As I continue my walk, the wind picks up, swirling leaves and snapping branches. Ants and snakes scatter across the path. My hair and eyes shift back to their normal colors as I push forward, finally reaching school.

At lunchtime, I share the money with my friends under the big mango trees. It fills me with a strange joy, this little act of kindness. In math class, a teacher asks if I want to join the school's dance competition. Excitement pulses through me, and my hair and eyes flash with that familiar color shift.

After school, my friend walks with me to the neighborhood's entrance. There, I spot a tall, light-skinned man coming toward me with tense, clenched fists. It's my father. As he approaches, I feel a chill and try to divert my path, but he calls out before I can slip away.

"Why are you coming home so late?" he says, adding, "I forgot to give you money this morning. Your mother has prepared your favorite meal." We walk home together, and as we enter, I see Mama in the kitchen, busy cooking for the family, who have come to visit.

After greeting everyone, I head inside to drop my things. My father follows and gives me instructions. With a knot in my stomach, I go to the kitchen, where Mama is working, and nudge the pot of sauce off the fire while she's distracted.

It spills, and I race back to his side. He grins, praising me, and hands me money for grilled fish and attieke.

Mama's voice trembles as she begs, "Why are you doing this?" Guilt churns inside me, but fear of my father keeps me silent. Being near him feels as unsettling as when the spirits come close. I have what other children might envy, but I am not happy. With rising anger, Mama calls on God, "The wind has neither shadow nor tangible presence—-that is God! I do what I do to please you."

"Let your God try to save you." My father's words linger as I lie in bed, unable to shake the weight of his disdain.

Three nights later, I leave my body again. This time, I travel farther, passing close to an airplane filled with people. I long to be inside it, to know what it feels like to soar with others. But I am drawn onward, arriving at a golden land so breathtaking I don't want to leave.

Back at home, my father grows harsher by the day. Each morning, his curses follow me. "You'll leave like your brothers," he sneers, trying to undermine Mama's belief in the vision she saw before I was born, reducing it to mere illusion.

CHAPTER 3

Understanding My Visions

At 4 pm on a weekend, I leave the house with plans to spend my money on snacks. On my way back, I spot a big brother from the neighborhood smiling at me from afar. A sick feeling twists in my stomach, and I feel my hair darken. In my vision, he splits in two—one part of him walks into the courtyard beside us, while the other, his spirit, veers into the cocoa plantation where young girls are taken to be circumcised. My sight follows his spirit as it moves deeper into the forest until it reaches a tree where he becomes bound, as if by invisible ropes. The sight makes me lose all appetite for the alloco—street-fried plantains with spicy sauce—that I had been carrying.

When I return home, Mama questions me about my untouched snack, but I only look away. At sunset, while I'm sitting by the well, another vision appears: a man, covered in blood and weeping, stands nearby. I glance toward Mama, busy in the kitchen, wondering why she doesn't seem to notice the disturbing figure. The next day, on my way to school, I spot another blood-covered man standing in the middle of the road, one foot broken. Cars pass right through him as though he doesn't exist. Horrified, I shout, "Look! Look!" but the other students see nothing. We continue down the road until, not much farther along, they scatter at the sight of a fresh accident. It's the same place where I had seen the man's figure moments earlier.

That evening, I finally tell Mama about the visions. Her response is swift and sharp: "Don't speak to anyone about what you see!"

A few weeks later, the community gathers in the public square to watch a woman perform a ritual to reveal the witches and wizards among us. She is an unusual figure—fair-skinned and toothless, with a body shaped like a guitar. To do her work, she dances naked to the steady beats of her muscular drummers. The entire village has come out to watch. At one point, the woman calls me forward, and a murmur rises from the crowd. She pauses the music, then looks at the people and declares, "Here is my boss—and yours." I lower my eyes, unsure if she really means me, and she gestures for me to sit by her side.

Then she summons the big brother I saw in my vision and asks for his name. She says to the crowd, "This one is bound in the bush. If I don't deliver him, he will be sacrificed." At her words, people begin to cry, begging her to save him.

She moves on, revealing a dark truth about the old woman who circumcises the girls. "She killed her only daughter in an accident," the woman explains, "and now uses a sharpened bone from her daughter's body to perform the rituals. The girls she circumcises remain childless and under her control." One by one, she calls the affected girls forward to deliver them. In the chaos that follows, I try to slip away, but I am spotted and quickly placed back beside her.

None of this is news to me.

Days later, while I'm running an errand to buy wine for Dad, the woman intercepts me near her house. She takes the wine from me and says, "Boss, go tell the one who sent you that I've drunk his wine." I return home and relay her message to my father, surprised when he doesn't react with anger.

Afterward, the woman leaves town, her mission completed. Not long after, the sorcerers she named begin to die, one by one. On Christmas Eve, the big brother, Chinal—the community's football team goalkeeper—returns from Abidjan. He brings me baked fish as a gift. He's a kind man, often sharing fruit or snacks with people around him.

But lately, a strange rooster has been causing trouble, knocking over our food and pecking at dishes. It stands apart from the others, refusing to crow at dawn. Instead, it shakes its head and stares intently into people's eyes. One day, I look directly at the rooster and see Chinal's face in its place. I tell him, "Big brother, the rooster is you. You should find someone to help you or else…"

He just laughs, brushing it off.

After Christmas, Chinal's sister, Mireille, runs ten kilometers to find me, pleading that I come with her to see him. When we arrive, his older brother is at his side, tending to a stove and carefully replacing the coals whenever they burn low to keep the room warm.

"You warned me," Chinal says the moment he sees me. His skin is pale and sickly, his eyes sunken and red. No one knew he was ill, as his father had kept him secluded indoors.

News of his condition stuns the neighborhood, and they urge his father to let him be taken to a hospital. His father refuses, but I also voice my concern, telling them that if any medication enters his body, he will die. Despite my warning, they insist, and he dies shortly after being taken.

At his funeral, I feel Chinal's spirit trying to speak through me, but I resist. Soon, his father turns his anger toward Chinal's pregnant sister, Sally, who had tried to find a cure for her brother and knows that their father is somehow responsible. He attacks her, and she tragically loses her baby, delivering a stillborn child. Grief-stricken, Sally and her husband leave the area to escape their father's wrath.

One night, as I look out over the soccer field behind our house, I see a strange figure—a man showering, naked, at the field's center. Each time he pours water from a bucket over his head, he shifts into a different animal. I recognize him as Chinal's father.

The next morning, around ten, I am at the market under a warm sun when, only a meter away, the rain suddenly begins to fall, accompanied by a fierce wind. The wind hurls an iron roofing sheet in my direction, hurtling toward my neck. The women in the market cry out, instructing me to drop to the ground. I obey, and the sheet whizzes past, barely missing me.

The women rush to my side, flooding me with questions. "Are you all right? Are you hurt?"

As they question me, my hair and eyes darken, and my insides roil like boiling water. A pregnant woman faints from the tension in the air, and they hurry off to get water for her, leaving me alone.

Later that week, the waders—a long-masked figure dancing from side to side—appear. Although I can't see his face, I know the masked figure is Chinal's father. He stops in front of me, his gaze drilling into the center of my forehead. My body feels as if it's melting under his stare.

Suddenly, I feel an opening at my back, as if a rush of air fills me from within. My hair gleams like gold, my insides bubble, and my feet lift off the ground until I'm eye-level with the mask. We lock eyes, and he stumbles back, collapsing to the ground. The drummers, singers, and onlookers scatter in shock.

"Go home!" he yells after me, his voice laced with anger.

The next day, I see him lying ill on a mat outside his door. He meets my gaze, and I feel his rage burning through his stare. I relish the sight, feeling proud of my newfound ability to defend myself. Yet, a part of me longs to understand and master this power so I can protect myself whenever I need it.

My Invisible Friend

I'm sitting in the backyard with a snack in my hand, but I can't bring myself to eat it. My hair turns dark red, my eyes deepen in color, and my stomach churns uneasily. Dad will be back from his trip soon, and I know it's about to begin.

They say a frog, when placed in comfortable water, doesn't notice the rising heat until it's too late.

Dust swirls around me as a snake suddenly darts in my direction, poised to bite. Before it can strike, a hen intercepts it, and the two animals begin a fierce battle. The snake wraps itself tightly around the hen, but she pecks and claws until she pulls herself free. She wins, and the snake retreats. The hen vanishes as quickly as she arrived, leaving me unsure of where she went or how she disappeared.

I walk to the front yard, where Mama is in the open kitchen. She asks if I'm all right, but I avoid her question, going straight to my room instead. Darkness fills the room, thick and heavy as if it wants to swallow me whole. My hair starts to shine, and my face glows with light. A voice, warm and steady, whispers, "Don't be afraid, I'm with you."

A few days pass, and Mama decides to make her palm sauce and tikritis—a dish I love. She asks me to fetch the leaves she needs to wrap them, which grow on a tree along the path to my school in the cocoa plantation. I hesitate; I don't want to go. But she has no one else to send, and I know the consequences if I refuse.

As I near the tree, the wind grows fierce, and a small whirlwind forms in front of it. I'm terrified but can't return without the leaves. I hear voices behind me and feel a glimmer of relief, but the people change paths, leaving me alone with the tree. It seems to be surrounded by a transparent bubble, and as soon as I cross that boundary, I feel my breath leave me. The whirlwind lifts me off my feet and throws me into the dry leaves. My throat burns, but I crawl toward the tree, desperate to complete my task and escape whatever spirit is bound to it. I climb, pluck the leaves, and dash home.

When I return, Mama scolds me, "You're so stubborn! Every time you bring those leaves, you've got sand in your hair."

That night, after dinner, the voice returns, instructing me to revisit the tree—just my spirit this time. I feel a force guiding me, and as I enter the cocoa plantation, my hair and eyes light up. I reach the tree and see a white cloth fastened to it. Inside the cloth are small, mysterious items: a white oval shape, kola nuts, a pebble, white powder, and a 1000 CFA bill. I see a girl trapped within the tree, screaming. The voice tells me to remove the cloth and scatter the contents, freeing her spirit. I do as I'm told, and since that night, whenever there is another victim, the voice guides me back to perform the same ritual.

Two days later, I visit a friend's house. As I approach, I see naked women running around in confusion, people singing, and others scattering in search of help. My friend's mother clutches her arms over her chest, and her father looks on, bewildered. I look around, trying to understand their alarm.

My friend stands at the doorway, her face ghostly pale, as if drained of all blood. She stares around like she's an alien seeing this place for the first time. A woman leads her to a chair and begins to feed her.

"Help!" the woman cries, "You were dead and have come back to life!"

Hearing this, I start to back away, but my friend calls my name, her voice desperate.

"Come!" she shouts. I point to myself to confirm she means me.

"Yes, you!" she says, waving me over.

A neighbor nearby adds, "Thank you. When she woke up, she said it was you who freed her from the trap." The people press around me, asking questions, and I try to crawl out of the crowd.

The story spreads across the neighborhood, and everyone questions me endlessly. One neighbor, who is like a father to me, smiles warmly whenever he sees me, though now I try to avoid him. One day, he catches me and says, "My daughter, you know your father is very mighty. But we men—all of us— are afraid of you."

"What does that mean?" I ask.

"Nothing. You'll understand one day," he replies with a knowing smile.

Now, whenever I walk through the neighborhood, people's eyes follow me, watching me as if they're seeing me for the first time.

At the dance circle, the rhythm of the tam-tam drums transports me, filling me with energy. Among the spectators, a girl keeps staring at me. I become irritated, assuming she's judging my hair. I walk over to her and grab her collar, tightening my grip.

A group of people arrives, trying to separate us, but I hold my ground, refusing to let go. "She said my hair is red," I insist. They glance at one another, murmuring in hushed tones, exchanging glances of doubt and confusion. The questioning continues, pressing me to describe the person who insulted me. I point, indignant, and say, "Yes! It's her!"

They respond, "It wasn't her who said that."

"How would you know?" I demand. "You weren't there!"

Together, they reply in unison, "It couldn't have been her. She's mute."

Embarrassed, I loosen my grip and let go of her clothes, pressing a few coins into her hand as a peace offering. Flustered, I dash home to Mama, arriving earlier than usual. She notices right away and begins peppering me with questions, knowing that I'd never leave the music early.

Before long, the girl's mother appears at our door, here to complain. But Mama stops her mid-sentence. "No need to tell me, my sister," she says, sighing. "She's done worse! Tied someone to a tree, broke her classmate's tooth, danced at school when she should've been marching." She asks forgiveness on my behalf, as usual, and then turns to me. "Don't do it again," she says with a stern look.

After my evening shower, while I'm putting on lotion, Mama corners me with a bamboo stick. When it breaks, she grabs another, and I scramble, running outside naked to save myself. Just then, Dad comes home, and an argument breaks out—he never likes it when she beats me.

That night, as I lay in bed, a cold light shines over me, making the room frigid and causing me to shiver. The floor beside my bed suddenly opens, yawning like a deep well, and I'm transported somewhere else entirely. I'm now among a group of young people gathered in the bush by a murky puddle. Their faces are unfamiliar to me, yet there's a chilling sense of purpose in the air. The group leader issues instructions, and one by one, they transform into reptiles, slipping into the puddle to fulfill their orders, only to gather again afterward.

Their task is to bite the youth in their reptilian forms, infecting them with spirits of addiction—to alcohol, drugs, violence, and lust. I spot the one responsible for killing and slap him hard across the cheek. He winces, feeling the sting but seeing no one, and continues his orders. In that moment, I find myself perched on a tree before them, my body radiating white light that pierces the darkness, illuminating everything around us.

They clutch at their faces, blinded by the brightness, crying out in agony as they struggle to shift back to their human forms. But they can't; the light holds them trapped in between, stripped of their powers, writhing in pain.

My light reaches even the smallest insect under each leaf. I don't want to stop, but the voice whispers that it's time to leave. Soon after I disappear, villagers find the group and call the authorities. They drape the culprits in loincloths, and the entire neighborhood comes to see the spectacle.

"Unbelievable! Never seen before!" the villagers murmur, gathering around. I stay at the edge of the crowd, watching from a distance. Suddenly, I catch the eye of the one I slapped; his gaze fixed on me, wide with awe and confusion. I turn and hurry away, knowing I've played my part.

As I enter our front yard, faint voices drift to me from within.

Taking Responsibility

"Hey, you! Where are you coming from?" Dad asks sharply. "Your mother says God sent you to be rich, and I agree. But as long as I live, you will suffer all your life." He curses me, punctuating his words with angry gestures.

"Every morning, it's the same words," Mama rebukes, her tone weary.

When he storms off, she turns to me and says softly, "Don't listen to him! You are a queen, sent by God to serve Him."

The next day at school, Moussa sneaks up and strikes me from behind, calling me every name he can think of and mocking my red hair. I lunge at him, digging my nails into his skin, especially under his eyes, until blood spills everywhere. Teachers arrive, peeling us apart, but I'm the one punished—the disgruntled director happens to be Moussa's father.

Moussa terrorizes everyone, knowing they won't fight back for fear of his father's influence. But I'm made to kneel until the end of the school day. When I get home, Dad notices my disheveled appearance and asks what happened. I tell him about the incident, and the next morning, he goes to the school himself. From my classroom, I see him in the courtyard, but he doesn't come in. Minutes later, cries erupt from all directions.

All the students and teachers gather outside. My dad stands over the director, who's sprawled at his feet, bloodied. He lifts the director by the collar, shaking him. A voice whispers to me, "The director will expel you, but don't worry."

Later that day, Mama arrives at the school, accompanied by several people, to plead with the director. "I don't want my daughter away from me. She's always sick, year after year. Who can take care of her like I can?" She speaks humbly, and with the support of others, he eventually relents. I am allowed to stay.

Two days later, a flood sweeps through the streets. Trees are uprooted, canopies and cars are tossed about, and visibility drops to barely fifty centimeters. Parents struggle to reach the school to collect their children, but the wind and water make it difficult. Cries and shouts fill the air as we push our way through.

As I hurry, my right foot slips out of my shoe. Knowing Mama would be furious if I lost it, I chase after it, but the rushing water sweeps me off my feet, carrying me and my backpack toward the lagoon. People nearby try to help, but the wind keeps them at bay. The lagoon's waters churn with broken bottles, pebbles, antlers, and other sharp objects. Yet, somehow, an invisible force keeps me floating right at the edge. After a while, rescuers arrive and pull me to safety. Around me lie the bodies of children and adults, twisted metal, shattered wood, machines, and animals. My dress is torn, but I'm unharmed. Only a few dazed survivors stand nearby, lost in disbelief.

Mama finds me, nearly naked, and clutches me tightly. Together, we comb through the wreckage in the rain, searching for anyone else. Soaked to the bone, we finally return home. Dad is waiting at the door.

"Where were you?" he demands. "You didn't see this rain coming? I told you not to let her go to school, and you ignored me! If anything happened to her, it's on you!"

Mama ignores him. "Go inside and change, then wash up," she says to me, her voice steady.

That night, I'm overcome by an unfamiliar sensation. My body feels heavy, my head spins, and I struggle to breathe. My hair grows darker, my stomach tightens, my chest aches, and my ears throb. I think of my friend, and immediately, the sensation lifts, leaving me free. In the morning, Dad scolds me for sleeping in. "Your mother says God sent you to be rich, but as long as I live, you'll suffer," he sneers.

After completing my chores, I return to bed, listening to the rain pattering against the roof. Strange images flicker across the ceiling like scenes on a television screen. I see shooting stars, and their light fills my room. Amidst it all, the voice whispers, "I am here."

Suddenly, I find myself among the stars. From there, I am whisked away to another country by an invisible hand. The next thing I know, I'm standing on a grand stage like a rock star, holding a microphone. A crowd stretches before me, filled with people of every race, gender, and background, even those battling disabilities and illness. The stage lights shine so brightly that every detail is visible, down to the smallest point.

The sound of the crowd swells, and my hair and eyes gleam with a golden glow. My stomach flutters with excitement, and I relish the feeling. As I open my mouth, healing energy flows out, words I don't recognize but somehow know. I speak hidden truths, and people begin to cry, collapsing under the weight of emotion.

I don't want to leave, but my friend says, "It's not time yet."

In an instant, I'm back in my bed, staring at the ceiling.

CHAPTER 4

The Rape Plot

One evening, I'm walking home from my cousin's house, which sits in a part of the neighborhood with dense forest and few houses. It's getting dark, and the animal sounds around me are unsettling. I quicken my pace, eager to get out of the trees. Just as I near the forest's edge, shadows flicker around me, and a young man suddenly jumps in front of me, blocking my path. My hair and eyes darken as three more men step out of the shadows and close in, surrounding me.

"Hey, Witch!" a boy shouted.

I noticed right away who he was. Not too long before, he sent me a letter asking me out on a date. I was embarrassed and showed my friends. What I didn't know was Zady would share that letter with the whole school!

I knew revenge was imminent.

"You think you can just laugh at me with your friends and get away with it?" he snarls, his voice low and dangerous. "Now we'll see who's laughing. The four of us are going to show you what happens to girls like you. And when we're done, everyone will know."

"Please, forgive me—I didn't mean to hurt you!" I plead, but they're unmoved. The director of the power company is nearby, and his security guard hears the commotion and starts toward us.

Thinking quickly, I try to reason with them. "If you're angry, let's fight. Hit me if it'll make you feel better!"

"No," they sneer. "We don't want a fight; that's why we brought knives."

"Let go of my hand!" I shout, planting my left foot firmly on the ground, trying to wrest my hand from his grip. When I can't break free, I clutch his shirt, refusing to let go. Just then, a man emerges from the bushes, striding straight toward us.

"Are you okay?" he asks, glancing from me to the young men. When I explain what's happening, he turns to face them, unshaken by their threats. "I'm watching you leave," he says simply. To my surprise, they back down, letting me walk past them without a word. After I get a few meters away, I hear cries behind me. When I turn back, the men are scattering, and the stranger who helped me has vanished.

The first day back at school after the weekend, I'm excited to see my friends under the big mango trees. But as I approach, they step back, watching me with wary eyes.

"Witch!" someone yells, but I ignore it. A stone flies past me, and insults erupt from all sides. When it's time to go inside, no one wants to stand in line with me—not even the teacher, who acts strangely.

The voice in my head whispers, "It was the young men who spread rumors that you're a witch." During class, the teacher leaves briefly and returns with the director, who calls me to his office.

Once there, he demands, "Why did you send demons to scare young people who did nothing to you? I'll be informing your parents." I stand silent, letting him finish. When he dismisses me, I return to class. On the way back to my seat, a crumpled piece of paper hits my back. Objects continue to pelt me whenever the teacher turns away, and laughter fills the room. I turn to see who's responsible.

After school, I catch up with her and ask why she's been doing this. She meets my eyes with a smug look. "Leave, or I'll change your hair color," she threatens. I snatch her school bag and fling it into the bushes behind us. The other students yell, "Palaver fight! Palaver fight!" egging us on to fight.

She's taller than me, so I strike her throat to bring her down, then grab her hair, pulling her head toward my knee. I hit the side of her face hard, and blood sprays everywhere. I don't stop until a teacher comes to break us apart.

When I get home, my dad asks about my backpack. Before I can answer, my mama says, "Your friends brought your bag here, and we want to know why." Dad, however, loses his temper, insulting me and blaming Mama for everything. Knowing he probably thinks I was careless with my things again, I keep quiet.

The next day, I'm summoned to the director's office again because the girl's father has filed a complaint. I explain my side of the story, and he agrees with me, though the director and others remain unsatisfied. Only one teacher defends me—the one who once told me I'd be rich one day because of my generosity. The story spreads quickly, reaching my parents, and Dad stands up for me.

As I walk home that night, a strange light fills my vision, and my hair and eyes shift color. Before me, a magnificent door opens, leading to a tunnel filled with a powerful whirlwind. I step forward, dressed in resplendent clothing that seems to shimmer in the wind, though I feel no rush.

In a flash, I find myself in front of the Hollywood sign, looking down at the city below. Slowly, I descend and begin walking among the people. Most don't notice me, but those who do seem uneasy, some even trying to get close. But flames surround me, keeping them at a distance no matter how they stretch toward me. The dogs on leashes sense me too, barking and pulling against their owners' control.

I savor the walk, reluctant to leave, but I'm aware I'm not in control of how long I stay.

Days pass after the first incident, and, at my mother's urging, I join a study group with a few young men. We start studying each evening at 9 p.m. One night, after a few hours, I notice the three of them exchanging signals—quick glances, barely-there gestures. The muscular one inches toward the door, and they start talking in low tones, their laughter forced and unnerving. Then, without warning, he locks the door, and the other two flank me, one on each side.

"Take off your clothes," they say, voices too calm.

I assess the situation and, heart pounding, I rise from my chair. I reach for the buttons of my shirt, pretending to comply. They ease back a little, relaxing, and one of them says, "Pick where you want it. The mat or the bed?"

"The mat," I answer. The muscular one moves to grab it, and that's my moment—I bolt for the door, bare feet pounding the floor as I race outside, leaving everything behind. Grabbing clothes from the line, I throw them on hastily and run home. Mama's face falls when she sees me.

"We're going to the deputy chief of police," she says immediately. He lives just across the street. It's 3:48 a.m. when he opens his door, listens to our story, and jots down notes. He sends us home with a promise.

The following day, while the men are in class, uniformed officers arrive and haul them to the station. For three days, they're disciplined with batons before being released.

A week later, on a quiet evening, I'm out walking with a young girl from our neighborhood. Something feels off; the night air is thick, and insects buzz louder than usual. People passing us swerve away as if repelled by an invisible force, but I can't hear anything clearly. "Let's head home," I say, sensing trouble. Before we can move, a group of high school boys appears, closing in around us, their faces lit with smug satisfaction.

"Got you this time," one of them sneers. "Because of you, our friends got beaten by the police. We'll settle that tonight."

They seize us, dragging us toward a nearby school. "Take off your clothes!" one barks, a command laced with malice.

"Please, let her go. She's innocent," I beg, but they just scoff.

"We don't care," they chant together like it's a game. Desperate, I say, "If you let her go, I'll do whatever you want." One of them raises a hand to strike me when suddenly, a man appears out of nowhere, wielding a thick piece of wood. With one swift motion, he charges toward us, and they scatter like leaves.

In seconds, everyone is gone. The man, too, vanishes into the night, and I'm left there with torn clothes and one broken sandal. I don't want Mama to see me like this, so I slip inside, relieved to find the door still unlocked—it never is until I'm back.

I reach the middle of the living room before the light snaps on. Mama's waiting, her gaze heavy, and I know there's no escaping the questions. I tell her everything, the words spilling out in a rush.

With a steady, emotional voice, she says, "I've always told you, you're here because God sent you. You came through us, yes, like every child, but you belong to Him. Strengthen your bond with Him—He's the only one who can truly protect you. Without Him, I'll lose you, and I refuse to bury any more children."

The Laguna Creatures

It's a scorching day as I walk toward Laguna Beach, passing through the cocoa plantation. I hear my name—softly at first, then multiplying, with voices echoing all around me. Sunlight streams through the trees, and birds fill the air with their songs.

My hair and eyes begin to change color, shifting like reflections in water. I pause for a moment, then continue, arriving at the laguna from behind. Young people from the neighborhood are already in the water, laughing and splashing. Since I can't swim, I hang back, gathering mangoes. As I pick the fruit, a heavy weight settles over me, and I feel rooted to the spot, powerless. I sense a presence nearby but keep my head down, unwilling to look. A strange force enters me, and I see a transparent figure with my face.

Among the swimmers, other translucent beings mirror the faces of those in the water. No one else seems to notice them. The figures look as if they're made of water. The one with my face smiles and walks past me as I watch. In my vision, these beings leave the plantation, transforming into real people. Even transparent cars appear, solidifying as they emerge. They're visible to everyone—tangible and real—but no one else sees where they came from. They drive away, and I am shaken by the vision as I make my way back through the cocoa plantation.

As I walk, I notice an old woman crouched, muttering to herself. She's the one who tracks wizards and witches for the neighborhood. I quicken my pace, passing by before she spots me.

A couple of mornings later, before dawn, the air thrums with the beat of tam-tam drums. I arrive early, finding a gathering already forming. Young girls, their bodies painted with intricate white kaolin designs, dance, while others cry in their mothers' arms. In the courtyard, women huddle in groups, chopping okra and potato leaves. Large pots bubble over wood fires, drums of palm oil line the area, and young men slice up goat and lamb meat.

Everyone moves to the rhythm of drums and songs. At one point, a woman takes one of the young girls by the hand, leading her into the bush. Moments later, a scream echoes, quickly followed by sobs. As the cries grow louder, the drummers pound harder, and the women's voices rise. One by one, the girls are led away, disappearing into the bush without returning.

Suddenly, a woman with tear-streaked cheeks emerges from the bush and shares news with a waiting mother. The crowd shifts uneasily. The drumming and singing quieten, and people in the courtyard abandon their tasks to press closer to the bush. Women arrive with their hands on their heads. Fathers gather, too, some holding cigarettes, others shaking their heads in silence. As I turn to leave, a door suddenly appears before me.

I'm transported to the bush, among the girls who were taken. They sit on the ground, except for a little girl lying on a mat, blood pooling between her legs. My gaze settles on her until another girl stands before me, tears streaming as she pleads, "Help me." I don't respond, frozen in place. The scene grows chaotic as adults begin to file in.

The drums fall silent. The old woman performing the circumcisions grips a sharp bone, her tool for cutting. Blood stains leaves, mats, fabrics, and the women's hands. The girls who've been cut cry out, their bodies coated in sand. The adults tend to the unconscious girl's wounds, chanting as they prepare a poultice. A voice within urges me, "Touch her," and I reach out. She sneezes, then coughs.

In an instant, like being sucked through a vacuum, I find myself back in the courtyard. One of the adults rushes in, singing and dancing. The noise resumes, the gathering swept back into celebration. I slip away, heading home to avoid any attention.

"You're home early. I can still hear the tom-tom," Mama says.

"I wanted to help you cook," I reply.

As we prepare the meal, women pass by our house repeatedly, each casting glances in our direction, as though searching for something. I duck inside just as a group from the gathering arrives at our home, their faces tense and troubled.

Mama asks them why they've come, and one of the women responds, "Is this child your daughter? There is a problem."

Mama frowns and asks, "What problem?"

"We enjoyed the celebration so much," they say, "that we want to offer to circumcise her, to keep her from chasing after men as she grows."

At this, Mama stiffens, standing like a soldier catching sight of a superior. "We're not from the same culture or the same place. How dare you come here with such a request?" she snaps. "Her father will be home any minute now, so you'd better leave before he finds you here." Her voice grows firm. "Get up and leave!"

Once they're gone, another group of women arrives, eager to convince her. "We didn't know she wasn't circumcised! Our daughters told us."

Mama, her patience worn thin, demands again that they leave our property. After they finally go, she mutters insults under her breath, then turns her attention to me.

"You! Come here!" she says sharply. "What did you do there?"

"Nothing, Mama!" I answer quickly. I'm thinking about retreating to my room when the voice speaks to me: *"You saw them, so now they want to take you from this earth. But don't worry, I'm here."*

The First Death

Tonight, the darkness is thicker than usual, and my room is the darkest of all. Shadows move within it, like a suffocating wind pressing down on me; my bones feel as heavy as lead.

In the stillness, Mama's chest continues to rumble, sounding like an old motor. The room is charged with strange forces, like a weight pressing on my chest. My lips feel sealed shut, my breath shallow, my legs rooted to the bed.

Suddenly, a rush of fresh air fills me, bringing strength, and the shadows vanish. I can finally rest, though dawn is already breaking. Mama calls me to go to the market, and I yawn constantly as I prepare the meal, my eyelids heavy with exhaustion.

I usually finish cooking in three hours, but today it takes longer. Mama sits across from Dad, watching me with a frown. The meal is ready, but I'm too weary to eat.

I head straight to my bedroom, but before I can fall asleep, I find myself somewhere else—a village square. I'm tied to a chair in the center, my hands bound behind me, my feet before me, and leaves pressed against my lips. A fire burns nearby, its light casting dim shadows over banana leaves that cover the ground. At the lake's edge, plastic basins are lined up.

It's so dark that the fire barely illuminates my surroundings. Men and women surround me, *and the only one face I recognize is Daddy's;* their knives glinting in the low light. They slice into my flesh, cutting as if it were fresh meat, each cut sending waves of pain through my body. My soul leaves my body and watches from above, writhing as my flesh endures the agony. Blood pours from every wound, covering it entirely. Just as darkness blots out my vision, I lose consciousness—and find myself back in my room.

Mama is eating, Dad reclines in his favorite chair, and children run through the courtyard, laughing and playing. I call out to Mama, but she doesn't respond. I reach for her shoulder, but my hand passes through her. Dad sits, his face glowing as he whistles along with the tune on his radio. I move toward him, but my feet don't touch the ground, and no one seems to notice me. It hits me—I'm a wanderer now, a mere ghost.

I try to scream, but my lips won't move. I'm lifted into the air, floating like a helium balloon, higher and higher until the earth becomes just a dot below me. I'm alone in the void, but then, a hand grabs me, pulling me back to the village square where they had cut my flesh. The villagers are dancing and singing, celebrating their victory.

They gather the pieces of my flesh in a basin, blood flowing across the banana leaves. I watch as the fragments of my flesh and blood begin to draw back toward me, my body slowly reassembling itself. And there, in the crowd, is my father, dancing with the same villagers who had torn me apart.

The hand holding me flings me back into my body, and like a shooting star, I'm hurtling back to earth, landing back in my room. My body is swollen, my lips too heavy to open. Half an hour later, I drag myself to the door of our house. I see Dad under the avocado trees, his face going pale as he spots me. He stands up, then sits down, only to jump up again, repeating the motion three times.

I'm frozen in the doorway, my strength spent. My senses are sharp, but my mind struggles to process it all. Mama notices his agitation and asks, "What's going on?" Dad breaks into a cold sweat, knocking over the dish on the stool before him. I'm parched, my stomach hollow, yet food has no appeal. He stares at me, unblinking. I meet his gaze, watching as his face flushes and his hands tremble.

I can't move any farther, barely able to stand. Mama finally notices me and rushes over as I collapse. She lifts me with shaking hands, offering me a cup of water. The taste is bland, and I struggle to swallow. Dad remains speechless, his mouth slightly open as he watches.

Soon, the sun changes color. I'm still lying in the living room, my senses overwhelmed by strange sounds and mixed odors. My body is both hot and cold, and my mind replaying the recent events. I know I'm here by God's grace alone. The day drags on, and slowly my strength returns, though my mind is still haunted by everything that happened.

Whenever I recall that Dad was there, my senses spin, and when I remember what he did, I'm overcome with torment. Days later, he corners me in the courtyard, his voice tense. "You run away from me?"

"No, Dad!" I reply, trying to sound casual.

But his narrowed eyes and stiff posture show he doesn't believe me.

Later that afternoon, my friend President—an old man, older than my parents—- stops by, telling his usual stories. As I see him off, he turns to me and asks, "What would you say to staying with my family for a while?"

His family lives nearby. "You must be joking," I say. "What could you possibly help me with? I told you I'm not leaving my country!"

We laugh, though my heart is far away, my mind turning over new ideas. I know I have to make a change, to take responsibility for what lies ahead with my father.

CHAPTER 5

The Challenge Between Dad and Me

The roosters sing, and as the sun appears, Dad's voice cuts through the morning air:

"God sent you to serve Him, but as long as I live, you will suffer! Your mother believes that some god spoke on your behalf, so you will never succeed. Look at your life—you hang out with the sick, the abandoned, the junk, and even those with Down syndrome, all the people no one wants, whom you've gathered over the years. I won't waste another cent on your education; I'll kick you out of my house until you follow your brothers' path!"

I stop in the courtyard and shout, "You said 'God'?"

"Yes," he replies, his tone seething.

"Then God is my father—you're merely my guardian on earth, nothing more!"

With that, I dart away as he chases me in a burst of rage, but I escape quickly.

At sunset, I sit behind the house in nothing but my underwear, my mind heavy with thoughts of how this so-called father has become a curse in my life. "Where are you? You only come when I'm asleep! Where are you?" My tears fall in torrents, streaming from my eyes, wetting my nose and mouth, pooling on my chest. My voice, deep and resonant like a foghorn, echoes across the courtyard. On my knees, with fists pounding the ground, I tear at my clothes as I cry out, "Where are you?"

When I lower my head between my folded knees, I whisper, "Why didn't you let me be with You at Your crucifixion? I wouldn't have betrayed You like the others did." These words have been my national anthem every December while watching *The Passion of the Christ.* Even as my hair darkens and my tears dampen my feet, I sense a presence calling my name—Mom.

She approaches, clad in her full loincloth, her eyes brimming with tears and her voice trembling as she says, "He won't do anything to you. Go take a shower—I've prepared your favorite dish." After crouching beside me in sorrow, she retreats to the kitchen.

I head inside, nearly colliding with Dad at the door as he stands aside to let me pass while still trying to hold me down. Later that night, as I lie in bed with my body lit by a wild internal glow, Dad shouts from his room, "I want to sleep in MY house—this is not your house!" His insults cascade throughout the house. In the darkness, I feel cockroaches scurry over my feet and mice dart beneath me. Suddenly, the roof trembles as a violent wind and thunder shake the building, their sounds mingling with Dad's relentless barrage. My body feels as if it's being crushed, yet my mind remains strangely detached, searching for the Spirit capable of splitting my burden in two. Like a tree rooted to the ground, I stand motionless while a chill runs through my hair and down my back, and lightning roars outside, shaking everything.

An insect crawls onto my head, and I quickly crush it between my thumb and forefinger. Meanwhile, Dad's angry shouts persist through the night. The house is filled with cousins, aunts, uncles, and students, yet none seem to hear the chaos around me.

With the arrival of dawn, I am exhausted but must sweep the yard. Dad—towering at 6'4", once a boxer and dancer with a surprisingly gentle singing voice—stands watching me from under the avocado trees. The neighbor's father, who has always smiled at me since I was young, calls out kindly. I drop my palm-leaf broom and step toward him, carefully descending the stairs Dad built to separate the courts. In my mind, I wonder, "What does he want from me?"

Near him, he speaks in a solemn tone, "Your father is strong and powerful; we are men, but we are all afraid of you."

"Why, Dad?" I ask.

"Oh, when you grow up, you'll understand," he replies.

I return to my chores, his words echoing in my mind. Suddenly, Dad emerges from somewhere, shouting for me to leave his house. His anger gathers the attention of people from neighboring courts. "I did not build my house to be a slave! I am free to do as I please!" he bellows. They exchange looks, eyebrows raised. The neighbor questions him, "What are you talking about?" But Dad continues, "I won't pay your school tuition anymore! Girls aren't meant for school! I sent you to school, and that's why you don't respect me!" One man protests, "But she is brilliant!"

"I don't care," he snaps.

Chaos erupts—voices shout, hands wave in the air. One man even offers to take care of my tuition, but Dad's fury remains unyielding. Old men, now part lawyer, part judge, display astonished expressions hiding secret smiles. I see surreal images—others crawling, some flying, some barking, even figures with horse legs or bear heads—exclaiming, "Bonnet blanc, blanc bonnet!"

Mom's eyes have been wet since morning, a silent testament to her worry over my future. My head burns, and my heart sinks, but my body remains still, while my soul clings desperately to the hope of light at the end of this tunnel. Yet, for now, I must go to the market.

On the hilltop, I pass torn shoes and faded black pants scattered in the brush by the roadside. Approaching, I see someone lying there—my friend "President," unconscious again. Known for drinking cases of beer and wild antics, he sleeps wherever the night finds him. I love him as family, so I rush to help him stand. "Are you okay?" he mumbles.

"Yes," I reply, urging, "Come on, let's go to the market. Can you walk?"

"Hum," he answers, weakly. His grey hair and wrinkled face bear the marks of many rough nights, but his spirit endures. In our conversation, I remind him, "You are richer than the president of this country." He laughs, patting my shoulder, and for a moment, despite everything, I feel a spark of joy amid the chaos.

My Father is a Killer

One evening, I ask my dad for my school fees.

He replies, "My daughter, if you're counting on me, you're not going to school this year."

I'm unbothered by his response, convinced he'll come through later. He's never denied me school before; in fact, he's always been a vocal advocate, challenging those who believe girls shouldn't be educated. But as the days pass, his words hold true, and he doesn't change his mind.

The first day of school arrives, filling the neighborhood with a unique energy. Parents, new and seasoned, bustle about getting their children ready. Students parade in crisp uniforms and neatly styled hair, eager for the new term. I, however, sit by my door, taking it all in, enjoying the day from the outside.

My group of friends stops by as usual, expecting me to walk with them. Their surprise is palpable when I tell them I won't be joining them this year. Voices are low with concern, they listen as I try to stay composed. After the tears subside, I urge them to continue, walking part of the way with them before heading back home.

On my way back, I'm surprised by classmates I've had quarrels with; they cry for me, expressing sympathy. But after a few days without a uniform, I become the shame of the neighborhood. My peers point fingers, whispering behind my back, while parents ask, "You're really not going to school anymore?"

Each morning, I watch former classmates taunt me on their way to school. It feels as if the stars themselves have fallen upon me.

My mama cries quietly in the kitchen. Watching me dress for school has always been one of her greatest joys, especially since she was forced to leave school at a young age. She's always dreamed of seeing me succeed, but my father refuses to let her have this joy.

"Mom, what are you doing?" I ask.

"Sit down," she says. "Look for a private school. I'll make soap, cookies, and rural foods to send you. There's a new school on the hill, far from here."

"I'll check it out and let you know what they say," I reply.

The feedback is positive, and soon I'm enrolled at Saint Cyrille High School. My cousin gives me some of her old skirts and new white blouses, and friends help with books. Even a few parents contribute supplies.

Things go well until one day, I'm summoned to the director's office for sitting on the hood of his car. After a bit of questioning, I'm let off with a warning.

Some time later, an educator pulls me aside and says I need to pay my school fees or stop attending. I glance at the paper on her desk and point, "But this isn't the usual amount."

"Well, that's what it says here," she replies.

I return to class, my heart heavy. How will I tell Mama? I sit, lost in thought, not wanting to burden her. My mood turns sour, casting a shadow over my entire being.

The professor calls my name several times, finally pulling me out of my thoughts. As the class leader, I'm asked to organize everyone before dismissal. But when I ask for quiet, Maryanne, a new girl, challenges me, "I won't be quiet. What are you going to do about it?"

Calmly, I write her name on a slip of paper and send it to management. Later, she threatens me, "I'll blacken your hair today!" I turn to her with a smile.

Our classmates signal for her to stop, but she ignores them. The final bell rings, and students crowd around, chanting, "Fight! Fight! Fight!"

She tries to intimidate me with her height and broad frame, but I don't hesitate. I grab her collar and pull her close as she yells, "Let go of my shirt!"

"Oh, you were going to blacken my hair? Go ahead, do it!" I taunt her.

Before she can respond, I slap her, then knee her in the face. Blood trickles from her nose as educators rush to separate us. Soon, I'm back in an office explaining what happened, and she is the one punished while I'm allowed to go home.

As I approach the courtyard, Mama greets me warmly. But when she notices the bloodstain on my shirt, her face falls.

"Did you fight today?" she asks, concern etched in her voice. She sits next to a pot of boiling sauce, her arms crossed and eyes weary. I stand there, not saying a word, before slipping inside to change out of my uniform.

The next day, another educator escorts me to the director's office. He sits behind his desk, wearing a white shirt and blue tie, and gestures for me to sit down with a smile.

I sit, sighing, already sensing the bad news he's about to deliver.

"How are you, Miss Genifere?"

"I'm fine, sir. And you?"

"I'm fine, but I'm afraid I don't have good news for you this morning."

He rises from his black leather chair and perches on the edge of his desk.

"You haven't paid your fees in a while," he says. "I won't expel you, Miss Genifere, but you're only allowed to return once you've settled what you owe." He hands me a piece of paper, and I leave the office.

Walking back to the classroom, my head hangs low. I drag my feet, delaying the inevitable, but eventually, I arrive. I pack my things, each item feeling heavier than the last, and begin the journey home, kicking up dust along the way. When I reach the house, I find Mama in the kitchen as always, her scarf tied around her head, and her wrapper tucked across her chest. She's stirring a pot of seed sauce.

Noticing my expression, she asks, "What's going on?"

I approach her slowly, leaning against one of the kitchen pillars. "They say I didn't pay the fees," I say, then slip inside without waiting for a response.

After changing out of my uniform, I return to help Mama in the kitchen. She's staring into the distance, seemingly unaware, as the sauce begins to boil over. A few moments later, she murmurs, "But isn't there still a little time before payment is due?"

I stay silent.

She straightens up and sighs. "I'll go speak with them myself."

The next day, I hurry over to my friend Emma's house. She attends a different school, but we're in the same grade. Her face lights up when she sees me, her light skin glowing. Her short hair is neatly combed, and she's already dressed in her uniform, which emphasizes her tiny waist.

"How are you, Emma?" I ask.

She grins. "What do we say?"

I get to the point. "Could I come by every night to copy the lessons from the day?"

"No problem," she replies without a moment's hesitation. "But why?"

"I'm no longer allowed in my school," I answer with a smile, trying to hide my worry.

On the way home, I break into song, singing and clapping as I dance down the path. I can't wait to tell Mama. When I share the news, though, she stays quiet, her expression pained. I pull her close, hugging her tightly.

That evening, as Mama begins to doze off in the kitchen, I encourage her to rest.

"Go back to bed, Mama. I'll finish everything here before I bathe," I assure her. As I gather the utensils to put away, a shadow darts toward me, crawling up to my left knee in a flash.

I shake my leg, and it vanishes as quickly as it appears.

My Mother's God

Every evening, I'm at Emma's house, copying her notes and asking questions as if I'm back in a real class. Her high school is just a block from my home, so sometimes, I even slip into her school through the unfenced side. Occasionally, I get caught, but I always find my way back a few days later.

For months, this routine goes smoothly. Then, one evening, just as I'm gathering my notebooks and pen to head over, my father's stern voice stops me in my tracks.

"Where are you going?" he demands.

"To my friend's house," I reply.

"You lie!" he snaps.

My face stiffens, but I meet his gaze without a word. His anger bubbles over, each insult landing with a force that fills the room. I move to sit beside Mama in the kitchen, and as soon as I do, his one-man tirade fades.

For the next few days, he's relentless, staying home and blocking me every time I try to leave for Emma's. One evening, a concerned Emma comes looking for me. She finds me in the kitchen, stirring a pot of placali, a thick cassava paste, while my father intercepts her outside.

"My daughter, are you the one giving lessons to Genifere?" he asks her.

"Yes, sir," she replies.

"Don't waste your time. She doesn't know anything. Your parents pay your fees because you respect them. Go home and focus on your own studies. Leave Genifere alone."

Emma stands there, visibly shaken. In a small voice, she tries to defend me, "But she's the one who helps me with homework, especially in math, algebra, and physics."

"I said go home!" he shouts.

I pause, my attention pulled from the placali as I watch Emma walk away. The spoon freezes in my hand.

"Are you trying to burn the placali?" Mama snaps, jolting me back. She offers to take over, but I refuse, determined to finish.

After dinner, I slip away to Emma's. I find her sitting on a stool with an attieke dish in front of her, flies hovering. Our eyes meet, and we both tear up, hugging each other for comfort.

On my way home, I notice a group of young people gathered, crouching over someone. As I get closer, I realize it's Natalie, my friend and former classmate, with Ali—a local boy who doesn't attend school—standing over her, fists raised, accusing her of insulting him. I step between them and help Natalie up, pleading with Ali and his friends to let it go. They refuse and threaten me instead. I take a stand, shielding Natalie behind me, but the tension thickens. Unable to hold back, I headbutt Ali. He stumbles, and his friends scatter. I unleash my anger, scratching his face until neighbors rush over to break it up.

Natalie slips away, leaving me to deal with the aftermath. Hours later, Ali's parents arrive at our house, furious. I explain my side to Mama, but when they question Natalie, she denies everything, leaving me alone to bear the blame. My father seizes the opportunity to shame me, and Mama denies me dinner. Feeling dejected, I slip behind the house, searching for the comfort of solitude.

I take in the fresh, calming scent of damp earth and watch the sun sink below the horizon, reflecting on everything that happened. Strangely, I feel no regret—only a sense of joy. I understand Natalie was afraid of punishment. Besides, it's not the first time I've been in trouble.

Chantal, another friend, once invited me to her grandfather's, and days later, her parents confronted me about missing money. I told them I hadn't seen Chantal with any cash, but suspicions lingered. Chantal was bold; she'd scale mango trees to share the fruit with me. She once led me to a cornfield, where we tore down scarecrows and drank the palm wine hidden beneath the palms. Her parents eventually saw me as a bad influence.

Even Natalie once stole a duck from Mr. Parker's caretaker. She recruited me and other girls to gather ingredients for cooking it, but when the caretaker noticed the missing duck, she pointed the finger at me. Mama whipped me that day.

As I gaze at the twinkling stars, I consider the source of all these misadventures, wondering why trouble finds me so easily. The sounds of children nearby break my thoughts. With a sigh, I realize it's time to go back inside.

Lying on my bed, I'm suddenly surrounded by shadowy figures, moving faster than the wind. Sleep deserts me, leaving only a single thought: to seek the God my mama always spoke of, the one she said had brought me here to serve Him. The silhouettes press down on me, heavy and ominous. My soul feels like it's slipping away, inch by inch, from my feet up to my chest. Just as it reaches my heart, something holds it in place—a barrier.

The shadows pull fiercely, trying to extract my soul, when a light brighter than the sun floods the room, piercing the darkness. A voice whispers in my ear, "I'm here! Do not be afraid."

Strength and joy flood my body. I'm in awe, captivated by the brilliance. The voice speaks again, "I'm Jesus Christ."

As this unfolds, my mama sleeps soundly in the next room, unaware. The fear drains from my soul, and the shadows dissolve into nothingness. In the light, a vision appears—a lake of fire, with ripples like waves rolling across its surface. It's both mesmerizing and painful to behold, piercing my eyes like needles.

The room is so brightly lit that even a needle on the floor would be visible. I cover my face with both hands, but the voice resonates in my ears, deep and steady. The intensity of the light, the power of the voice, the sensation coursing through me—all of it is overwhelming yet strangely bearable.

I'm lost in the experience, but as it slowly fades, I begin to process what happened. I collapse onto my bed, filled with a sense of celebration. My face glows, my heart races, and I feel a deep joy bubbling within me. My mind replays my mama's words, a comforting reel I can't shake. The light has vanished, but I'm left with questions—questions that will keep me awake through the night. Or so I think. My eyelids grow heavy, pulling me down toward sleep.

CHAPTER 6

The War Begins

I grab a broom and begin my morning chores. My dad passes by, then suddenly stops, staring at me with a puzzled look. His mouth isn't moving, but I hear his voice as if it's inside my head: *Why's she laughing?*

Mama arrives behind me, silent, but I can hear her thoughts too. *What is happening to me?* I wonder, but there's a strange thrill in it. My senses feel heightened, as though my eyes see farther, details sharper, and every sound around me amplified.

After sweeping, I head to the shower, but a voice warns me I'll have an accident if I do, so I change my plan. Later, as I walk to the market, the same voice warns of a snake. I slow my steps; moments later, a snake slithers across my path.

That evening, I have a vision of my dad in his room, shifting forms. His spirit leaves his body each night to roam the compound, joined by dark figures—his "colleagues"— who shed their skins and transform into creatures. Muscles and tendons exposed, they morph into reptiles.

Suddenly, I'm transported to a forest. People with faces marked by black paw prints gather around an elder sitting by an altar smeared with blood. Dressed in African cloth bound like a crown on his head, he chants as the ground fills with bowls and cowries. It's dim, the trees thick and towering, shrouding the sky.

Hiding behind some brush, I watch. A fire bursts into life, and a soul steps from the flames. Then, a snake slithers out from behind the tree and transforms into a young man from my neighborhood. Nearby, a lake shimmers behind the altar. The gathering speaks in a strange language, but somehow, I understand every word. Each holds leaves and horsetails in their hands as they begin dark rituals.

Those who kill hold a carved figure smeared with black paste inside a small coffin, calling out their victim's name before burying the coffin. They dance and sing, sealing the person's fate. Those who cause alcoholism pour alcohol over a statuette's mouth while chanting a victim's name. Those who break up couples use a stinking rhinoceros beetle wrapped in a lemon. They inscribe the couple's names on the beetle's leaf and bury it, while a statuette of the couple tied with string stands nearby. Over days, the lemon rots, the smell worsens, and the couple's relationship unravels.

For sterility, they have other methods: a snake swallows an egg in a female figurine or liquid leaks from a male one. They chant, arranging twisted unions, even sibling marriages. Some cause accidents, job losses, or drain young people's motivation for school. They impose spirits onto souls, caging them together until the person's body obeys the imposed spirit. At one point, they summon people's souls, locking them away.

It's as if an interpreter speaks directly into my ears. I feel myself among them, yet hidden. One of them senses my presence, turning his head, and then glancing at the others.

Suddenly, the elder rises, and I'm sucked back into my room as though through a vacuum.

The sun rises, and I return to my chores, sensing someone watching me. I turn to see my dad in the kitchen. Every time I look his way, our eyes meet before he quickly glances away, shifting in his chair. The sand piles up between his feet from his constant shuffling, and I can hear his thoughts: he's wondering if he really saw me at the meeting last night. His demeanor is quieter, his movements more cautious.

Throughout the day, he's distracted, and I enjoy watching him squirm. I move with confidence, my head held high. At dinner, I place his food in front of him without a word. His eyes question me, but I don't respond. Mama returns from visiting a friend, and I chat with everyone—everyone except him.

A few days later, I start feeling unwell. Before sunrise, I vomit and have no appetite, even for my favorite dish. My stomach churns, my head throbs, and I can barely stand. That evening, as my sickness worsens, Dad asks with a smile, "What's wrong?" He's been in high spirits all day, playing music and even laughing. Mama answers for me as I continue retching. The nausea and pain intensify, and my fear of needles keeps me from going to the hospital.

In the dead of night, the air grows thick, and shadows gather around me. I feel like I'm pinned under bricks, suffocating. One shadow, resembling me, starts emerging from my body—its head from mine, its hands from mine. But when it reaches my heart, it stops, stuck in place. The shadows pull and tug, trying to extract it, but they fail. My limbs are heavy, my eyes wide open, and a single sentence echoes in my mind: *Save me, God!*

Before dawn, the shadows finally vanish, and I'm left gasping, feeling the quiet of early morning return.

I Have to Use My Gifts

The fight with the dark shadows lasted several days, and I only began to recover when my mama gave me a concoction of boiled leaves. In my heart, a single phrase kept repeating: "Save me, God!" Afterward, I stayed home to rest a few more days before deciding to visit my girlfriend, Emma.

The neighborhood feels empty, but the aromas from kitchens drift through the air, and I hear the faint sounds of animals roaming. Small whirlwinds form around me, and a voice from the wind speaks to me in a language I don't know—yet somehow, I understand. Soon, the whirlwinds encircle me while everything else stands still.

I sense my hair and eyes changing color, though my heart feels strangely calm. Walking feels heavy, and the sun's heat scorches my skin more intensely than usual. I feel a presence around me, though I am physically alone, so I start singing a hymn I learned in church that speaks of divine protection. As I sing, a surge of strength rises within me, sharpening my senses.

I notice people staring: a man lingering by his door, a woman who had just been sweeping her yard, others frozen like statues. Their intense gazes unsettle me, but I continue toward Emma's.

Suddenly, a commotion erupts nearby. A group of children is chasing my old friend Basayi, who, as usual, is stumbling around drunk. The children mock and taunt him, so I shout, "Leave him alone! He's old enough to be your father!" The children scatter, and I help steady Basayi, letting him lean on me as I lead him home. His house isn't far, just a short distance from mine. I decide to return home instead of continuing to Emma's. As I approach the house, I hear my parents' voices raised in argument.

"We'll never get along because you can't support my decisions!" my father shouts.

My mama crosses her arms, lips pressed tightly together. Though I've seen them argue before, the tension today feels different. I sit outside, feeling my heart race as a few neighbors gather to watch. They ask my father what the fight is about, but he doesn't answer, only repeats his accusations.

Then, suddenly, silence falls. Their voices fade, and I find myself enveloped in an eerie stillness. I can see their lips moving, their hands gesturing, but no sound reaches me. A strange light surrounds me, and within this bubble, a voice whispers, "He invites her to join him in eliminating you." In that moment, I understand the true cause of their conflict. When sound returns, I quietly slip away to my room. I lie on my bed, feeling sadness rise within me, and I murmur, "God, save me."

Time passes without my realizing it, and soon, night falls. In the darkness, I feel them come again—shadowy intruders filling my room. My limbs feel weighed down, but I manage to rise and call out to God. This time, they vanish faster than before. I stay awake until dawn, finally closing my eyes when morning arrives.

After a while, I hear Mama's voice urging me, "Get up to sweep and go for a walk. It's late!" Reluctantly, I pull myself out of bed. I encounter my father in the living room and mutter a greeting, but he ignores me. Just as I reach the door, I feel a sharp blow to the back of my neck. When I regain consciousness, I'm lying on a mat, surrounded by familiar faces. My father is nowhere to be seen, and Mama's face is streaked with tears.

"How long was I out?" I ask, but no one answers. Faces filled with questions hover above me, and someone finally asks the crowd to give me space. The neighbors step back, and I pull my loincloth tighter, shivering under the warmth of the sun, chilled despite the heat.

My father arrives, shirtless and barefoot, demanding, "What happened?" The crowd starts to disperse, but one neighbor quietly leads Mama inside. Meanwhile, my father and his companions—pretending concern but truly his spiritual allies—exchange knowing glances and whispers. Sensing something wrong, Mama quickly returns to my side, but my father tries to block her path. Others intervene, and she finally reaches me.

"You need to go to the hospital," she insists.

"No! No, I don't want to," I protest.

She pulls the loincloth aside, revealing my shivering, fevered body, as weak as a soaked chick.

At the hospital, perched on a hill, nurses bustle around with trays holding large metal syringes. After a quick examination, the doctor decides to give me a dose of Quinimax, a drug known for its pain, high mortality rate, and the risk of disabling the patient's foot. I cling to Mama, screaming as the doctor calls for reinforcements. Two men grip my arms and legs while another holds my torso, bracing me as the needle plunges in, my cries echoing through the building.

I'm resting in a hospital room when my mama offers to carry me on her back. She's of modest height and a bit overweight, and her movements are unsteady under my weight. We slowly make our way down the hill as cars drive past in the opposite direction. There's no paved road, just tracks over the grass. Suddenly, a car honks at us, startling Mama. In her hurry to move aside, she trips on a pebble, and we tumble down the hill, rolling to a stop at the feet of herbs. The car drives off, leaving us stranded without help.

Mama struggles to crawl toward me, and as I look at her, a wave of pain fills my heart. We're like two hippos caught in the mud, and my face is covered in dry leaves. I whisper, "Help me, God," and feel a warmth surge through my limbs, like electricity. My hair changes color, and I hear a gentle voice say, "Get up." Leaning on my arms, I slowly rise to my feet and move toward Mama.

"How are you, Mama?" I ask.

Our eyes meet, and she stares at me, wide-eyed, her mouth slightly open in shock. As I help her to her feet, her hands tremble, but I gently brush off the dry leaves clinging to her clothes and hair, ignoring her murmured protests. I check her over to make sure she isn't hurt, and then, hand in hand, we begin the walk home. Though her gaze remains filled with wonder, I can tell that, to her, the most important thing is that I am well.

Being Proactive

Sometime later, a stranger with bright eyes and a blazing smile appears in our neighborhood. He lives in the compound next to mine and often stares at me with a curious intensity. As I pass by, I greet him out of courtesy, but nothing more. Mama has already told me he's a laborer from another country, and I'm not interested in getting to know him.

One evening, as I return home from a walk with my girlfriend, she stops to say hello to him. I refuse to join her, but he calls me over. Out of respect for my elders, I reluctantly approach, meeting his gaze directly.

"Are you well?" he asks.

"Yes," I reply, keeping my tone curt.

He tells me my mother has a kind heart and that, because of this, he wants to help me. He suggests I buy a red rooster so he can perform a ritual to make me rich. Although I try to hide my disbelief, I can't help thinking he's absurd— especially when he adds, "God has already made you rich; the rooster will only activate it."

"I'm not interested," I respond bluntly.

As he speaks, the wall behind him fades away, revealing an eerie display: cowries, a small wooden statuette of a woman, and a black animal skin, all arranged under a spiritual veil that stretches from floor to ceiling. In front of the statuette lies a plate with silver coins, a mat, and a wooden board inscribed in Arabic. Nearby, I see the stool he likely uses to summon spirits.

Physically, I stand before him, but my soul seems to drift around his room. He raises a portable camera, trying to snap my picture. I refuse, but he snaps one anyway, placing the camera back in his room. However, when he returns, he finds the camera smashed. By then, I am already walking home, and he chases after me, shouting that I broke it. I know I didn't touch anything; I only probed the spirit he worships. His accusations hang in the air, but I start singing hymns from the Esterre congregation, which I find both therapeutic and protective. Eventually, he stops, though I can still feel his gaze lingering on me from afar.

Later that evening, my dad arrives with a friend, only to find the man reporting me. Without hesitation, Dad tells him to leave, and the man slinks away like a sheep facing a bear. Mama suggests Dad should report him to the landlord instead of confronting him directly, but Dad brushes it off. As his temper rises, I decide to slip away before he directs his usual outbursts at me.

The next morning, Dad's friend, who spent the night, leaves early, taking some of our belongings with him and leaving the door wide open. We wake to Dad's shouts, echoing through the house. I can't help but find it a bit amusing to imagine Dad sneaking things out of the house himself or involving an accomplice.

Later, at midday, we gather under the avocado trees to eat, grateful for the shade in the scorching heat. Suddenly, a naja snake falls among us, causing everyone to scatter, flinging utensils in every direction. My poor mother trips, the stool trapping her foot in her haste to flee. I run toward the kitchen, which is quite a distance away, while Dad grabs the nearest object—a plate—and turns to confront the snake. As he waves the plate at it, the snake rears up in defense. A neighbor joins the struggle, brandishing a large piece of wood. The snake wraps itself around the wood, tightening its grip.

More people arrive to help, but the snake's speed and aggression make it difficult. It eventually releases its hold, spits at the crowd, and slithers quickly away. Someone hurls a piece of wood, striking it, and the snake, now enraged, turns on its attacker, scattering everyone once more before retreating into the bushes.

Once the panic subsides, laughter erupts as people tease those who ran. I begin gathering the scattered utensils when I notice blood on my arm. I'm puzzled, as I hadn't fallen or been touched by anyone. I recall only a sharp pain when the wood hit the snake.

I rush to Mama, exclaiming, "Mama, look! I'm bleeding!" Concerned, everyone quickly offers advice and theories about my injury, leaving me overwhelmed. When they bring out alcohol to clean the wound, I slip away, pretending to fetch something inside. Behind the house, I grab a handful of sand, rubbing it on the wound until the bleeding stops.

A few days later, a tall, beautiful woman with light skin arrives at our home, escorted by a neighbor. She carries two large bags, and the man leading her uses a long stick to steady himself. I'm sitting in the courtyard and quickly rise to help, noticing the man's exhausted expression. When Dad sees the woman, he freezes, his eyes wide, mouth agape. I call out to him, but he doesn't respond, so I focus on the visitors, offering them water as is customary.

Dad remains visibly shaken, but Mama greets the visitors warmly, trying to make sense of the situation. Her voice seems to bring Dad back to reality, and he finally manages a greeting.

The woman announces she's looking for a man named Bessou. That's my dad's name. The neighbor explains that he'd seen her waiting by the roadside and offered to help when she mentioned Dad. Mama and Dad thank him, offering him food before he departs. They extend the same courtesy to the woman, but she insists that she only wants to see the person she's seeking.

Dad steps forward, identifying himself, but the woman shows no excitement at finally meeting him. Dad's face tightens, and he seems unhappy about her presence. I carry her bags to a room in the flat next door. She declines food or a shower, wanting only to rest. When I bring her a lamp, Dad stops me, leaning in to whisper, "She can't see. What does she need a lamp for?"

Realizing he was right, I set the lamp aside. Meanwhile, Mama is in high spirits, thrilled to have a guest. After pressing Dad with questions about his unease, he eventually confesses that he thought this woman had died over twenty years ago. Troubled, Mama asks, "Are you sure?" I quietly turn my thoughts to God, seeking His help. As their conversation continues, Mama's laughter rings out intermittently, mocking the strange turn of events.

"I'm serious," Dad says. "She's several years older than me." Her youthful appearance suggests otherwise, but he seems certain.

That evening, Dad stays outside until very late. Surprisingly, the night is peaceful—no unsettling encounters or strange occurrences disturb me. The next morning, I wake up feeling cheerful, humming a song as I rise. When I enter the living room, Dad rushes over and says urgently, "The woman is sitting by the road. She wants you to take her to the clergy, but tell her no."

Instead of heading straight to meet her, I take the path behind the courtyard, hoping to avoid his watchful eyes. Assuming I'm just wandering off to the neighborhood, he doesn't pay me any mind. From behind the courtyard, I make my way to the road, where the woman sits beside her luggage, her cane resting in front of her. She perks up at every sound— the crunch of dry leaves under my feet, the chatter of passersby.

"My daughter, is that you?" she asks, her voice tentative but hopeful. I crouch down and move closer, careful to stay out of sight of my parents.

"Yes, ma. I will accompany you," I reassure her softly.

"God bless you, my daughter," she replies, her tone lifting with excitement.

We set off toward the Catholic Church of Saint Augustine. The journey is long and tiresome. After about thirty minutes, her breathing grows labored, and the weight of her bags feels heavier in my hands. I suggest we rest and ask if she's had anything to eat. She shakes her head—no food, no water this morning.

Luckily, a young woman hawking baka—soft rice with sugar or condensed milk—is just a few meters ahead. I call out to her, intending to buy food, but the woman interrupts me.

"I'm not hungry," she insists. "I just want to see the l'abbe at the church. It's for him that I'm here. I haven't seen him in a long time."

"Ma, we still have more than three hours of walking to do," I remind her gently, concerned about her stamina.

She wiggles her head stubbornly and says, "Let's continue now."

The sun grows fiercer as we trudge along, the tar on the road softening under its heat. In my heart, I repeat, *"God help me,"* over and over again.

"If you are tired, leave me here," she says abruptly, scratching at her body. The sudden motion throws us off balance since we're both holding her stick. The road, strewn with stones, demands my full attention to keep us steady. My silent prayer continues: *"God help me."*

At last, we reach the parish. I help her onto a pew before heading to inquire about the man she wishes to see. No one recognizes his name or even knows of such a person. The questions rain down on me, but I have no answers.

Eventually, one of the sisters accompanies me to speak with the woman. When questioned, she gives nonsensical replies, dodging every inquiry. Her only insistence is that she not return with me. Frustrated, she lashes out, and the sister, looking resigned, tells me, "We will take care of her. You can go."

Relieved, I nod my thanks and leave. *Thank goodness,* I think as I make my way back home.

That night, as I prepare to sleep, a strange vision overtakes me. A screen appears before my eyes, and suddenly, I'm in a theater, watching a vivid scene unfold.

The screen shows a village, its people working in their plantations under the hot sun. My father appears among them, his presence inexplicable. A tall, dark man wearing only a loincloth strikes two long tom-toms, their deep sound reverberating across the fields. Villagers gather from all directions, interpreting the message carried by the drums.

I watch in confusion as my father assembles a group of young people and leads them toward a lake. The remaining villagers scatter—some returning to the fields, while the women throw themselves to the ground, wailing.

At the lake, Dad gestures toward the water, instructing the youths to dive in. Two of them plunge into the lake, while the others stand back, giving directions. Children cling to their mothers, frightened and confused, while the villagers who stayed behind hastily return with tools.

The divers resurface empty-handed. On their second attempt, Dad dives in alongside them. Minutes pass before he emerges, holding a body.

The villagers erupt into cries, throwing themselves to the ground in despair. They take the body from him, their grief palpable. Dad dives back into the lake, searching for the second body. With no firefighters nearby—the nearest town being 250 kilometers away—the villagers have no choice but to rely on my father's courage.

When he resurfaces with the second body, the villagers lift him in celebration, their cries of mourning replaced with shouts of gratitude. The bodies are carried to the chief's house, and just like that, the vision ends.

I find myself back in my bedroom, shaken.

The next morning, Dad shares a story with us. "When I visited the village a couple of weeks ago, my nephews drowned in the lake. I was the one who found their bodies," he says quietly.

He explains that the boys were siblings, university students visiting from Paris. As Dad speaks, a chilling voice whispers to me, *"Your dad killed them."*

The accusation shakes me to my core. That day, I felt out of balance, fumbling through my chores as if it was my first time doing them. All day, I avoid my father, unsure of what to believe.

As the sun dips below the horizon and the moon takes its place, unease settles over me. I wonder what the night will bring.

CHAPTER 7

My Second Death

Days turn into weeks. At the end of the third week, as the sun sets and my feet touch the courtyard ground upon returning from my girlfriend's house, I notice a gathering under the avocado trees. Dad sits shirtless in his usual chair, looking comfortable and relaxed. Next to him is a young girl about my age. Her light complexion, thin frame, and innocent face would catch anyone's attention.

She sits with her hand resting under her chin, her elbow propped on her knee. Between her legs is a small cloth bag. Mom sits beside Dad, her expression firm, while a stranger speaks to them. Without saying anything, I walk past the group and into the house.

Before I can disappear completely, Dad calls my name. I turn to see him gesturing for me to come over. "This is your sister," he announces, his voice steady and serious, like when he discusses work with his business partners. "Take her things and show her to the room next to yours."

The man explains her situation. He found her sitting by the roadside, crying. Curious, he approached and asked what had happened. She told him her brother, a soldier, had chased her out after catching her in his bed with a man. He refused to let her return home. She has no one in the city, so the man brought her to us, knowing we share the same language.

I can't help but smile as I meet her eyes. "Come on, let's go to your room," I say warmly.

Once in her room, we talk as if we've known each other forever. The days pass smoothly. She wears my clothes, and we become inseparable. My friends quickly become her friends, and she fits seamlessly into my life.

She's been here for over twenty days now. This morning, I wake up feeling unwell. My body burns with heat, and even my favorite dishes are unappealing. I take a mat outside to lie in the sun, hoping it will soothe me. The sun's warmth feels good against my aching body, but my symptoms persist. My urine is an alarming yellow, and Mom tries herbal remedies that have worked in the past, but this time, nothing helps.

Martine, as she calls herself, does her best to assist me, but my condition worsens. My weight drops, my tongue turns pale and white, and my eyes are as clear as egg whites. I pray to the One who promised He is always with me, but the heat in my body doesn't relent. My nights are haunted by spirits who approach me on my mat.

Before they can overpower me, I hear a voice warning, *"They're coming."* I cry out in my heart, *"Save me!"* Suddenly, I'm floating above houses and trees. My feet stretch out, spanning over thirty kilometers, and when I try to move, everything around me shifts. The spirits retreat, and I shrink back to my normal size.

The next morning, I finally agreed to Mom's suggestion to visit the hospital. "We'll go tomorrow," I tell her.

At 9:00 a.m., Martine and I set off for the hospital. The walk is grueling; I can't manage more than a few meters without needing a break. We pass landmarks that I usually admire, like Mr. Sibi's large, well-kept house with its gray walls, high fence, and vibrant flowers. Today, though, everything feels different. The wind tosses me around like a leaf, and every step is a struggle as I walk past the area of my attempted rape.

By the time we reach the hospital, we're exhausted. After waiting two hours to be seen, the nurse asks for my hospital book. "Oh, I forgot it," I mumble weakly.

We make the long journey back home to retrieve it, and then back again to the hospital. Just as we near the road leading to the hospital, right by Mr. Sibi's house, I feel a sharp blow to the back of my head, as if struck by a rock. The world spins, and before I can comprehend what's happening, I collapse.

My head lands on the ground, tilted to the side. My arm is twisted beneath me, and I'm half-lying on my shoulder with my legs folded awkwardly. I see myself sprawled on the ground.

Martine sits nearby, perched on the grass in front of the gentleman's house. Her expression is blank, void of concern or alarm.

A car approaches, and I wave desperately, but it speeds past, swerving to avoid my body. Another car follows and does the same. My surroundings shift, and suddenly, I'm on a cassava and yam plantation. I see a man napping in a chair near a small red-clay hut with a straw roof.

I try to call out to him, but no sound escapes my lips. Desperate, I cry, but even my sobs are silent. I step closer, stumbling over yam mounds and cassava stems.

"Good evening, sir," I finally manage to say. "I'm thirsty."

A woman emerges from the hut and tells me firmly, "Go back to where you came from. It's not your time yet. We have no water or food for you here."

In an instant, I'm back beside my lifeless body. A crowd has gathered. A man kneels beside me, checking my pulse. He shakes his head and solemnly announces, "She's dead."

"No, I'm here!" I shout, but no one hears me. People scatter, running in every direction—some toward my house, others to fetch help. Martine remains motionless, showing no reaction.

When I return to my body, I open my eyes to chaos. People scream and cry while Mom and Dad rush toward me. Weakly, I sit up and turn to Martine. "Why didn't you help me?"

She shrugs indifferently. "I thought you were playing."

Her lack of remorse stuns me, but I'm too weak to argue. Mom embraces me, her face wet with tears. Dad's calm voice cuts through the noise. "What happened?"

The crowd erupts, each person offering their version of events. Overwhelmed, I let them take me home. I have no energy to protest. All I want is to lie down and sleep.

My Dad Killed Me

Dad returned from the village earlier this morning. It's now 7:00 p.m., and we sit around him to eat from the same plate outside the door.

In the village, his two nephews, home from France for the holidays, went fishing but never returned. As the sun set with no word from them, concern grew. The villagers eventually called firefighters from a city more than 100 kilometers away. But with help far off, the villagers mobilized for a search.

Dad, however, entered the lake alone and found the boys' bodies submerged beneath the water.

"Your God wasn't there," he adds, recounting the event like a general reliving his war exploits—his posture proud, his chest lifted, his face alight with intensity, his voice smooth and commanding like a jazz singer.

Sitting nearby, his wife responds in a soft, childlike voice, as if asking for a favor, "God works in many ways. Even what you just described is part of His power."

As Dad speaks, I can't help but stare at him, something that always irritates Mom. Suddenly, it's as if a screen opens behind his head, and his voice fades into a hum in my ears.

On the screen, two young men walk along a gravel path that cuts through a tranquil lake. Flowers line the lake's edge, and in the distance, a dam looms. Across the water, a village rests atop a red-earth hill, where sheep, goats, and chickens roam freely. Women pound plantains under a tree in front of a modest home with a nearby kitchen and a cemetery in the back. A blind woman sits quietly in a large courtyard, her face turned to the sun.

The young men appear again, this time in a canoe. One wears a white tank top, the other a polo, both dressed in shorts. They chat and laugh as they fish, occasionally looking up at birds gliding overhead. But then, the wind picks up, and the lake's waves grow restless. The once-clear water turns dark and turbulent, thrashing the canoe.

The boys stretch their arms as though reaching for safety, but their efforts are futile. A sudden whirlwind engulfs them, and I see figures in the water—spirits of the wind and waves—upend their canoe. The boys struggle, their arms flailing and their legs weighed down as if chained. Air bubbles escape their mouths until they stop moving, their wide, terror-stricken eyes frozen. The spirits drag their bodies together beneath the lake, where they lie still.

The lake calms. Small puddles rise briefly, and from them emerge five figures, fully clothed and carrying machetes, as if untouched by the water. They disperse in different directions, except for one figure who resembles Dad. My thoughts seem to draw him closer until I'm certain it's him.

The vision shifts to the village. A tall man, barefoot and shirtless, beats a pair of large tom-toms with vigor, summoning the villagers. The drumbeats echo, and the people rush from their homes in all directions. Women throw themselves to the ground, their cries piercing the air, while men clutch machetes and sprint toward the fields.

Dad leads a group of young men toward the lake, his voice steady yet commanding. Babies play in the sand, confused children cling to their mothers, and the elderly shuffle out of their homes to watch. By the lake, men dive into the water, searching for the bodies. They return empty-handed, their expressions grim.

Finally, Dad dives in. Minutes later, he emerges with one of the boys' bodies. The villagers wail and collapse to the ground. Undeterred, Dad dives again and retrieves the second body. It isn't until then that the distant firefighters arrive.

The scene fades, and I see myself walking with Martine toward Sidi's house. Dad, trailing us unseen, strikes me on the back of my head with a black ball. Like the wind, he retreats to his body, now sitting in his chair at home.

Back in our courtyard, he speaks to a small tree that barely reaches my knees. He's surrounded it with iron buckles and tied a weathered vine between them. Pouring alcohol onto the soil around the tree, he murmurs as if in prayer. The tree has been there for over two years, yet it hasn't grown. Whenever Dad eats, he sets a small offering by its base.

In a flash, his voice snaps me back to reality.

"Bring me some water," he says.

I hand him the water and step away, uneasy but silent.

Morning comes, and I'm still in bed.

Dad tries waking me up to buy bread, but I squeeze my eyes shut and fake a loud snore. He mutters something before leaving the room, sending someone else for the errand. Once I'm sure he's gone, I get up and head outside.

Of course, Mom is waiting, ready with her scolding. "The sun is already out, and you're just now stirring?" she snaps as I busy myself under the avocado trees in the yard. My thoughts keep drifting to last night's events.

I glance toward the kitchen where Mom is working, wrapped in her colorful three-piece loincloth, her expression like a storm cloud. I know I'll have to make things right. Dragging my feet, I approach her.

"Mom," I ask hesitantly, "can your husband swim?"

She doesn't even look at me as she continues her work. "I don't know," she says curtly, then adds, "You heard him last night, didn't you?"

I nod, standing there with a broom in hand, swaying like Stevie Wonder. "Do you believe him?" I ask again.

Before she can answer, Dad strides into the kitchen, his steps hurried and close together as he checks his watch. Without a word, he disappears into his room, only to reappear moments later.

"Have you seen my blue folder from yesterday?" he asks Mom. She shakes her head slowly, elbows resting on her knees. Turning to me, he raises an eyebrow, waiting for an answer. I just stare back.

Frustrated, he turns to Mom. "You say there's a God? Where is He when I make you do whatever I want?" His voice is heavy with sarcasm and sneering pride.

Mom straightens, meeting his gaze. "The wind passes by," she says softly. "You can't see its shadow, or where it comes from, or where it goes. That's God. Don't worry, don't rush. One day..." Her voice trails off, firm but calm.

Dad waves dismissively and leaves the kitchen.

Later, Mom and I are pounding fufu under the avocado trees. The mortar and pestle clatter rhythmically as she turns the plantains into a smooth dough. From up the hill, I see Dad and his friends approaching, laughing and talking.

"Mom, your husband is coming with his friends," I warn her. "I hope there's enough to feed them."

"Oh, it's nothing," she replies with a gentle smile. "I'll give them my share."

Her hands move deftly, serving each dish with a grace that defies the urgency of the moment. The plates pile up in her hands, and she balances them expertly as I struggle to keep up. She turns to me, her eyes sparkling like polished marbles.

"Hurry!" she says, but when I try to comment on the foam rising in the soup, she cuts me off with a sharp smack to my leg. "We don't talk about it! You'll spoil it!" she scolds.

Once the food is served, Dad sends me to buy wine. When I return, he's in the kitchen, noticing that the portions were more than enough for everyone.

Looking up at him, Mom smiles gently. "It's God," she says simply, continuing to serve. Dad snatches the wine and storms off to his friends.

I head to my room, but one of Dad's friends calls me over, speaking with such kindness it takes me by surprise. He asks why I've been avoiding my father, but before I can answer, Dad interrupts.

"She's been avoiding me for days," he says with mock exasperation.

His friend asks me again why I've been distant. I shift nervously, my fingers in my mouth and my feet fidgeting. Dad's voice fades into the background as my thoughts drift.

When his friends leave, Dad confronts me behind the house, anger flashing in his eyes. "Why is *he* your friend?" he demands, referring to the man we all call President.

"He's not like us!" Dad's voice rises, his finger jabbing the air near my face. Mom steps in, her voice calm but firm. "We're all human," she says. "No one is superior to their neighbor. We're all created in God's image."

Dad's laughter is bitter. "I wasn't created in any god's image!" he scoffs. "If there's a God, why does He let me suffer? Why does He make me look crazy in this town?"

I feel a wave of nausea as I realize he's been feeding President leftovers and wine when I'm not around.

Later, Mom calls me over and invites me to sit beside her. "I'm proud of you," she says, her voice soft but certain. "Wherever you go—among friends, at work, in your community—you must do your best. Always. Be so good that when you're absent, people will say, 'If she were here, she'd do it better.'"

Her words fill me with a bittersweet pride. I nod, but my mind drifts again to a world I dream of—a world far from here, full of joy and possibility.

My Disappointment

When morning comes, Dad wakes me up to go buy the bread. I close my eyes and mimic a loud snore, a mocking "dong" escaping my lips. Frustrated, he leaves to send someone else. I hear him say he's going out—and that's when I finally step outside. Of course, Mom is already scolding me because the sun is up before I am.

Under the avocado trees in the yard, I begin my chores, but my thoughts keep drifting back to what I saw. In the kitchen, Mom—her hair a wild tangle, her beautiful camisole and matching loincloth draped with care—stares at me with clear contempt. I understand then; I promise myself, "I'll fix it." I trudge up the steps until I reach her side.

"Mom, can your husband swim?" I ask, voice uncertain.

She replies sharply, "You heard it last night, didn't you?" As she stands in her little pantry, broom in hand, I sway my head like an American Stevie Wonder before continuing, "Do you believe what he says?"

Before she can answer, Dad appears with quick, measured steps, glancing at his watch as he slips into his room and then back into the kitchen. While he approaches Mom, I move in the opposite direction.

"Yesterday, I had some papers in a blue folder. Did you see them?" Dad asks Mom. She shakes her head, her movements precise like a tennis referee, elbows resting on her knees. He then turns to me, asking in a hushed tone, "You say there is a God? Where is it when I do as I please?" His words drip with irony and sneer.

Mom retorts calmly, "The wind passes—you do not see its shadow, nor know where it comes from or where it goes! That is God. Do not worry! One day, you'll understand."

With a dismissive gesture, Dad swings his hand away and continues on.

That afternoon, Mom and I pound the plantains behind the house. We make a paste—a sort of doggie, as we jokingly call it—using a piece of dry wood with a hollow inside as our pestle. Another tool, heavy like an iron bar, is used to flatten the sand for our mortar. I stack the mashed plantains while Mom turns our mixture into a smooth mortar. Suddenly, I notice Dad arriving with his friends, walking down the hill.

"Mom, your husband is coming with his friends," I call out nervously. "I don't know if you'll have enough to feed them!"

"Oh no, it's nothing! I'll give them my share," Mom replies with a broad smile. Soon enough, with bread in hand, Dad and his friends settle happily, chatting about their football team. One of them even thanks Mom for preparing the meal.

Meanwhile, Mom and I continue pounding our mixture until it's time to serve. She serves with eyes that shine like marbles, moving faster than before. I try to speak—complaining about the foam on the sauce—but she abruptly hits my leg. "We don't talk about it when it's like that. You talked too much; it will stop," she scolds in a high tone.

Before I can finish cleaning up, Dad sends me to buy wine. I gather everything in my arms and head to the shop just outside the yard. When I return, I find Dad in the kitchen while Mom continues serving the sauce. He notices that the meal isn't enough for everyone, and Mom meets his gaze steadily. "It's God," she says softly before resuming her work. Dad snatches the wine and marches off to join his friends. I finish sweeping the yard and retreat to my room.

Later, one of Dad's friends calls me with great affection, asking if I want to eat before entering the house—but Dad quickly overrules him, grumbling that I haven't wanted to come near him for days. The uncle then questions me about my recent behavior. I stand there with my fingers in my mouth and my feet restless, glancing up now and then. Dad paces between the kitchen and his friends, his voice mingling with laughter around the dish of foutou as everyone praises the meal.

His wife sits alone in the kitchen, eating slowly. Suddenly, I hear my name from the yard—my friend "President" is calling. I rush out so he won't bring me bad luck. With a wave of his hand, he follows me behind the house. His steps are unsteady from a lingering alcohol smell, yet somehow he manages to stand. His pants and shirt always seem too big for him. He laments that he dug a hole in a corn plantation behind his unfinished house to hide his money, only for the rain to wash away the sand markers. He hasn't eaten since morning. I reassure him before heading back to the kitchen to retrieve my dish.

Dad watches my every move, his eyes following me. His wife, aware that he only comes to eat or ask for help, beckons me. She places a dish on the far side of the kitchen, and I snatch it quickly. I wander around the adjacent building, lowering my head to find him. "Take your time," I tell him, even as he offers me advice while eating, causing the food to spill. I sip water from a bowl near my right foot as his curved back leans over the dish, continuing to chat. At one point, he comments on how rich I look with so many people around me following my directions. But all I care about is leaving this place behind.

Dad's friends begin to gather, and I grab one of them's hands. "Let's go quickly before they catch up with us!" But President is too slow, and they notice. Dad shouts something behind the house, and his friends ask him what he's doing there. He remains silent until, upon returning, the chaos resumes. Furious that President is my friend, Dad nearly touches my forehead with his finger. His wife intervenes, reminding him that we are all human, created in the image of God and that no one is superior. But Dad sneers that he was not created in the image of any god. "If there really is a God, why do I suffer like this? Why am I driven mad in this city?" he exclaims.

My stomach churns as I struggle to hold back the urge to vomit, especially since Dad gives food and wine when I'm not around. My face crumples, my eyes wide with dismay. Mom stares at me, urging me to come closer. I drag myself to her, and she invites me to sit beside her. "I am proud of you. Wherever you are—in your friends' company, at work, in your community—people will speak of you in your absence. Do everything so well that when you're not there, they say, 'If she were here, she would do it better.'"

I listen, but my thoughts are far away, lost in another world of joy.

CHAPTER 8

Accepting Jesus

The sun has risen, and the moon has retreated. Today, Mom craves tikriti. The burgundy-red and deep-green leaves, plucked from the tender tips of branches, are prepared either alone or in palm seed sauce. These young, sticky, and fragrant leaves are my favorite. We eat them at least sixteen days a month, folding them into the sauce midway through cooking and letting them soak before removing and returning them. The reddish hue of the palm seed sauce, with its oily sheen rising to the top, is a feast for the senses. Paired with banana mess, today will be delicious.

At 9:00 a.m., I head to the tikriti tree to gather the leaves. The grass rustles around me, and the cocoa tree branches sway in the morning breeze. Suddenly, I notice movement—Uncle, who lives behind my friend Martine's house, is picking leaves. His frail frame floats in his oversized clothes. His collarbones protrude, his lips are dry, and his hollowed eyes give away his poor health. He glances at me and attempts a weak smile.

As I stand frozen on the path, the wind begins to howl, and the sky darkens. Across the road, I hear voices. A group of women carrying wood and machetes walks through the cocoa plantation, their heads shielded by an untouched blue sky. But here, the wind intensifies, whipping through the trees. Dead leaves swirl in the air, and Uncle loses his balance, clutching a tree for support. I want to help him, but my body refuses to move. His trembling figure struggles to stay upright as my thoughts spiral with questions.

Finally, I force myself forward, but the grass tangles my feet. Stumbling, I grab a branch for balance, my shoes sinking into the sticky, dark ground. When I look up, Uncle has fallen. He struggles like a snake on the ground before managing to stand. Relieved, I continue toward the tikriti tree. Yet, as I approach, an eerie sensation washes over me. I am not alone.

The air around me shifts, and suddenly I am inside an oval-shaped enclosure, like a glass shell within another. I can see the outside world—the trees, the lizards, the insects—but I am trapped. The air grows thin, and all I can hear is the sound of my own breath. My limbs feel heavy and unresponsive. Panic sets in as the ball tightens around me. In desperation, I call out silently, *God, help me!* At that moment, the shell shatters, and I collapse to the ground, gasping for air.

The dark sky clears. Covered in sand and dry leaves, I struggle to my feet, leaning on the tree trunk for support. Slowly, I climb to the branches and gather the Tikrit leaves. My hands overflow with them as I make my way home. Along the path, I see Uncle sitting outside a house. He nods weakly, signaling he's okay.

When I arrive, Mom scolds me for taking so long. I rush to rinse the leaves and mix them into the sauce. The aroma fills the kitchen, announcing our tikriti feast to everyone. Mom steps away to tend to something else, leaving the final steps of the preparation to me. I finish cooking and serve plates for Dad and the rest of the family.

This experience has haunted me for years, but I've never told Mom. She wouldn't understand and might never let me go gather leaves again. Yet, this morning was different. As soon as I called out to God in my heart, I found myself free.

Thoughts of this moment linger as I go about my day. I've noticed that when I hum hymns or ask for help, things seem to get easier. This morning, I feel like a bird singing with pure joy. The sun's rays pierce the sky, and I'm filled with an unusual energy. My favorite outfit waits for me, and I feel like I'm walking in the presence of greatness. In my mind, I stand on a podium, delivering a speech to a captivated audience. The world feels limitless.

With my chores done, I waste no time. I set out to join those gathering in a building to worship their God—a God who, this morning, I believe saved me.

My Relationship with the Holy Spirit

On the way, I feel invincible. I bound forward like a lamb, carefree and energetic. I hardly notice the sweat trickling down my face or the dust clinging to my feet. From a distance, the sound of music and voices captivates me, urging my steps faster. Others are running, eager to reach the same destination.

At the door, a young woman and an older man stand as greeters. The man wears a jacket, though his hair is disheveled, and his posture suggests weariness. From afar, their eyes meet, and they glance toward me. Immediately, I hesitate, considering whether to turn back. But I press on, stepping onto the first stair with my head bowed. The woman averts her gaze as I approach, but the old man acknowledges me with a subtle nod. Keeping my head down, I continue past them, crossing the threshold into the building.

Inside, I notice all the women have their heads covered and are dressed in full loincloths. My own attire—a pair of short pants and a sleeveless camisole—stands out starkly. Those who hear my steps turn to look at me with disapproving expressions, and I suddenly understand the woman's earlier reaction. Self-conscious, I sit on the nearest bench to my right, as far from the front as possible.

The music stops, and a heavy silence fills the space. I feel grounded now, as if my earlier sense of invincibility has vanished. The greeters enter and close the door behind them. Anxiety knots in my chest, and I long to leave, but there's no discreet way to slip out. The old man takes a place beside the one speaking at the front, delivering a message in a neighboring dialect that I barely comprehend. My head grows heavy, tilting awkwardly to one side, and I lie down on the bench. The cries of children wake me, and I see everyone outside, gathered around a black bull tied in their midst.

The speaker from earlier holds a container of liquid, accompanied by elders from the community. He speaks, though I catch only fragments of his words. When he finishes, he pours the liquid over the bull, and suddenly, flames leap into the air. The bull thrashes, and the crowd erupts into shouts of "Hallelujah! Hallelujah!" Their hands rise toward the limitless sky as they sing. Overwhelmed, I quietly slip away, unnoticed in my departure.

My shoulders sag, and my steps drag as I make my way home. My chest feels heavy, burdened by an invisible weight. I absentmindedly sweep leaves and pebbles from my path with my feet, taking far too long to reach the next block. The sun scorches my skin, but I continue on, lost in thought. Then, suddenly, a song catches my attention. It drifts from a villa, its melody penetrating me as I draw nearer. Brass bands, drums, and a bass guitar accompany the singer's voice. The only word I recognize is "Hallelujah," but the music moves me deeply.

Before I realize it, I'm swaying to the rhythm, and a small crowd gathers around me. Parents and passersby smile, handing me small bills. The commotion draws the homeowner out, clapping his hands and motioning for his family to join. More people come to watch, their curiosity piqued. I lose track of time as I dance, immersed in the music. Eventually, I notice my shadow has shifted—time to move on.

At home, my mother greets me with a stern look. "Where were you?" she asks, her tone sharp. With sparkling eyes, I reply, "I went to visit the One you always tell me about." She pauses, then laughs, gesturing for me to sit beside her. Her voice softens as she looks around, ensuring privacy before speaking.

"How was it?" she asks.

I tell her everything—well, almost everything. Some details I keep to myself, unsure how she might react. She nods thoughtfully. "I told you, it's because humans come from human that is why you came through me, but you belong to God. If you want your life to shine, you must hold onto Him. He sent you to proclaim His name to the world. One day, you will disappear, and when you return, the world will know that someone extraordinary has come back to this country."

Her words settle over me, as familiar as they are profound. I've heard them many times before, yet each telling carries the same weight of emotion. She recounts her vision with vivid detail, her voice changing with each scene, her hands moving expressively. Her eyes close occasionally as she speaks, hymns and soft dances punctuating her story. Tears mix with smiles, a testament to her unshakable faith.

That night, as I lay in bed staring at the ceiling, her words replay in my mind. "If you're here, show yourself," I whisper to the darkness. At first, there's nothing. Then, a ball of light appears where my eyes are fixed. It moves like waves on the sea, filling the room with an undeniable presence. I feel its warmth, though no figure emerges. My reflection in the light startles me—golden hair, radiant skin, and a smile worth a billion dollars. In that moment, I feel connected to the stars and the moon, as if this celestial experience is not new to me.

The next morning, I test this presence. Washing rice, I murmur, "If you're here, finish cooking this." To my amazement, the rice turns out perfectly, better than I've ever prepared it. From that moment on, I invite Him into all my tasks, feeling His guidance in everything I do.

One day, walking through the cocoa plantation, the familiar darkness and unease creep in again. With quiet confidence, I say, "Chase them away!" It feels absurd, like a child relying on an invisible protector. Then, I hear a gentle, soothing voice in my mind: "Say only my Name."

"What name?" I ask aloud, my voice trembling.

"In the Name of Jesus Christ," the voice replies. I repeat the words, and immediately, the oppressive atmosphere lifts. The sun shines brighter than ever, and the path before me is clear.

Attending Church

Sometime later, my feet scraped against the small stones scattered along the path. Yellow and green mango leaves carpeted the ground under the brilliant sun. With my head held high, my eyes pierced through the sun's rays as I made my way to visit Big Sister Esterre. But she wasn't there, so I continued up the hill toward Saint Augustine, where I had once accompanied Mom.

The grand house, usually bustling with people, was eerily empty. Outside, the singers stood in their uniforms. Children my age sat in groups on benches behind the building, surrounded by statues of saints—men and women of the Bible. On one side were the apartments for women, who wore beige outfits that covered them from head to toe. Across the road stood the men's quarters, similarly dressed but without veils. Helping girls from other regions, not in uniform, handed out books that began with Genesis and

114

ended with Revelation. We were instructed to read and ask questions.

Our leader gave us a peculiar direction: "Open the book and read the page it falls to. That's where your question will come from." When my turn came, I opened the book, and my eyes landed on a passage forbidding the representation of heavenly things on earth through statues. It also warned against depicting God through earthly images. I raised my hand to ask my question. The girl leading the session stared at me, her gaze stripping me bare, before retorting, "I'll call the Sister."

Moments later, a woman draped in the same beige attire arrived, exuding a forceful, intimidating presence. "Who asked the question?" she demanded. "It was me," I replied firmly. Like the girl before her, her eyes burned into me, her face twisted with disapproval. "I'll get the Father," she said, leaving with the first girl.

When our leader returned, she carried a large bag filled with sweets. She handed them out to everyone except me. Determined not to be overlooked, I approached her. "You didn't give me any," I said. "I already did. What do you want?" she replied dismissively. Stunned and embarrassed, I froze momentarily before returning to my seat under the weight of everyone's stares, their muffled laughs filling the air. My head sank into my arms as tears streamed down my face, soaking the bench and my legs. My fingers clenched tightly, and my feet, unconsciously scraping at the grass, tore it from the earth.

Soon, she returned, pretending nothing had happened, laughing and teasing the others. She handed out cookies selectively, her actions taunting those of us she ignored. Then, as she walked away, my eyes fixed on her feet, and without thinking, I willed her to trip. She stumbled, hitting the cement hard. Silence fell over the crowd as passersby and women in uniform rushed to her aid. At our table, faces once wet with tears broke into smiles. But inside me, a conflict raged—a battle between satisfaction and guilt.

I slipped away unnoticed, my feet carrying me to the city's botanical garden. Under the shade of bamboo, I sat, replaying the scene in my mind. A soft, disembodied voice whispered, "I didn't give you this gift to use it like that." Startled, I looked around. No one was there except for a small lizard climbing up and down a stalk. The memory of her fall played before me like a movie, and I lowered my head in shame. Gripping a stick, I began tracing lines in the dirt.

As days passed, the songs I had heard in the first congregation became my hymns. Yet, silhouettes of my past danced before me, haunting my nights. One evening, as I wrestled with my thoughts, a refreshing breeze swept over me, filling me with an eagle-like strength. I rose, determined to worship like the people I had seen, pouring my heart out until dawn.

Mom remained oblivious to my spiritual struggles; her attention was always elsewhere. Once in bed, she seemed to vanish—transported to Gagnoa by the comforting drone of the diesel motor she so loved, her snores echoing through the night. On the third day of the week, I longed for the congregation again, eager to draw closer to the divine. When she called me—"Genifere! Ge-ni-fere!"—I leaped out of bed, eager to prepare. Mom seemed excited, unconcerned that her meals might be late because of my plans.

At the congregation, I found myself surrounded by women veiled or dressed in vibrant fabrics, and men in crisp shirts and jackets. The preacher spoke in their tribal language, which, fortunately, I understood. Despite recognizing many faces, no one greeted me or offered me a seat. Only the children I attended school with acknowledged me. Their choir was vibrant and rhythmic, the drums and songs stirring something deep within me. Yet, I left without knowing the preacher's message or which book he had read from.

By midday, I wandered again, my heart still searching.

CHAPTER 9

Daddy Does Not Want Me to Go to Church

The wind blows steadily, carrying a refreshing coolness. The sun's rays soften under the gentle waves of air, and families, dressed in vibrant loincloths, stroll back to their homes after their congregations. My black scarf, tied neatly on my head, flutters slightly in the breeze, and I occasionally break into short sprints while walking. The flowers along the path seem to smile at me, and my face beams in return.

I wear a tailored pair of pants made from traditional fabric, paired with a fitted top that hugs my frame. The route to our home passes through a neighborhood of grand but abandoned villas, now inhabited by rats, agoutis, squirrels, and snakes. From afar, I see Mom seated in her outdoor kitchen, stirring a pot. Then I notice Dad approaching her. The atmosphere shifts instantly—I brace myself for the inevitable drama.

I greet Dad politely and move closer to Mom, who hands me two warmed dishes from yesterday's meal. She instructs me to set the food on the small table under the avocado trees for Dad. With a calm and measured tone, he asks, "What took you so long?" Before I can answer, Mom interjects from the kitchen, "She joined the worshipers today!"

Dad's face tightens, as though he's been forced to swallow a sour lemon. He takes a few spoonfuls of food and then gestures for me to sit beside him. Adjusting his position, he begins to speak:

"I know your mother makes you believe in some so-called god, but let me tell you, it's all nonsense. The idea of God is just a story made up by white people."

He continues with his theory, explaining how different cultures have their own gods—Chinese, Japanese, Indians—and claims that Africans have their gods too. My face remains attentive, but inside, my mind is swirling with questions. If our tribe alone has over ten gods, which one created the heavens and the earth? Which one made me in their image? I dare not voice these thoughts, but both Dad and I know the truth.

Finally, he stops talking, and I quietly clear the table. He watches me, squinting as though scrutinizing my every move. The afternoon sun casts shifting shadows around me, making me momentarily dizzy.

Mom leaves to check on her sheep, which have just given birth. As I stand by the coal stove, a wave of exhaustion overtakes me, and my body begins to sway like a crumbling structure. Just as I'm about to fall, Mom rushes in, catching me around the hips. Her momentum nearly topples us both, but she steadies herself against one of the wooden posts of the kitchen.

"Are you just going to sit there while the child collapses?" she snaps at Dad.

He dismisses her with a careless comment about being asleep. Mom offers to finish cooking while I lie down on the mat near the house door. I close my eyes, but strange visions flood my mind—black figures encircling me, only to vanish as I regain strength. Each time they appear, I feel an inexplicable surge of power, as if I transform into something indestructible before returning to my normal self.

Mom's unease grows. She refuses to eat or drink, keeping her focus entirely on me. At last, she steps outside, retrieves a bowl of trash, and heads to the road. When she returns, she's accompanied by two men and a woman, all holding Bibles.

"Please pray for my daughter," Mom pleads.

I sit at their request, answering a few preliminary questions. Then, they begin to pray. One of the men, dressed in a black vest, raises his voice, speaking in an incomprehensible language. The others respond with affirmations of "In the name of Jesus Christ."

From his spot under the avocado trees, Dad watches with a mocking grin. The prayers grow louder, and the noise overwhelms me. I shift uncomfortably until Dad interrupts, "Hey!" His sharp tone startles the group, causing the two assistants to pause, though the man in the black vest continues.

"Stop it, all of you," Dad commands as he strides toward us.

The man doesn't flinch. With closed eyes and one hand raised, he continues his fervent prayer.

"I told you to leave!" Dad barks, waving them off with a hand gesture.

Without argument, the group bids Mom and me a subdued goodbye before departing.

"I've told you before," Dad says firmly, "they're all liars, only after money. I don't want to see them here again."

Mom, visibly upset, turns her back to him and returns to the kitchen. Dad sinks back into his chair, his eyes fixed on me, scrutinizing me in silence. The tension in the air is suffocating.

"You bring them here again," he warns, his voice low and menacing, "and I'll throw you out of this house."

Climax

The next day arrives, and it's the same routine. My body shivers like a wet chick left out in the cold. Food holds no appeal; I can't even bear the thought of eating. My intestines churn, and my skin is riddled with goosebumps. My palms are pale, almost white, and I sit weakly on the mat outside, under the soft warmth of the sun. My body feels feverish as if my head and torso have become a furnace. My complexion is dull, like tarnished jewelry, and I can barely open my eyes.

Suddenly, darkness envelops me. I hear the faint sounds of children playing behind the house and my mother's commanding voice rising above all others. Yet it feels distant, as though the moon and stars are hovering just above my head. I can't see anything, only feel—hands striking me from all sides, like raindrops falling relentlessly. Strange shadows, sharp and fleeting, dart past me. They shrink and twist, moving at a speed I can't comprehend.

I try to grasp my reality. Mom usually calls my name for every little thing—so why can't I hear her now? I no longer feel the wall supporting my back or the mat beneath me. I am in another realm, drowning in darkness, as shadowy figures deliver blow after blow, raining down from my head to my feet. My legs stretch unnaturally, growing impossibly long, and suddenly, I'm in a surreal place where the sky meets the sea. Humans look like tiny chicks from my towering vantage point. The shadows that attack me are vacuumed into the ether, vanishing in an instant.

Next, I find myself amidst a group of dancers. A man sitting in the locker room gestures for me to show what I can do. I feel weightless, flying like a bird in a Hollywood scene. A brilliant light descends from the sky, wrapping around me. My heart races as my hair and face sparkle like diamonds. My skin transforms into crystal, my eyes into gleaming marbles. Journalists clamor around me, snapping photos, shouting questions, and chanting praises.

"You're the best actress!" one cries.

"No, the best dancer!" another exclaims.

The crowd sings my name as shooting stars streak across the sky. My white fur coat drapes elegantly over my shoulders, trailing behind me like a royal cape. Walking the red carpet, I'm the center of attention. Hands reach out to touch me, but none succeed. Cameras flash like fireflies, capturing every step I take.

Suddenly, I'm on a massive stage in a football stadium, a microphone in hand. My voice flows effortlessly, speaking words I've never studied. The choir behind me is immense, over a hundred singers strong, their harmonies filling the air. Each note from the band resonates with newfound energy.

My cassock shifts colors—blue, purple, and white—matching the divine truths flowing from my lips. Compassion swells in my heart. Miracles unfold before me: the wheelchair-bound rise, the deaf hear, the blind see. Tears of joy stream from those experiencing color for the first time. Sweat trickles down my glowing skin as I lift my hands, filled with a spirit far greater than myself.

A bright orb of light hovers above the crowd. I keep repeating the name of *Jesus Christ*. Then, in a flash, I'm pulled away and transported elsewhere.

Exhaustion overtakes me. I'm on the run, fleeing across rocky terrain and dusty paths. Sandals barely protect my feet as I stumble forward, pursued by countless faces—bureaucrats, traders, athletes—all united in their mission to capture me. It's as if they communicate telepathically, driven by a single goal: to deliver me for a reward. Even those too afraid to help me chase me away. The ground beneath me becomes hostile, and every step is fraught with danger.

The scene shifts again. I am in a war zone, planes raining bombs on the earth. Flames erupt everywhere, consuming all in their path. People scatter in terror. Some climb stairs that vanish beneath their feet, while others flee to mountains that crumble into the ground. The cries of men, women, and children pierce the air, unbearable in their anguish. Blood flows like rivers. Babies are forced from their mothers' wombs, their tiny bodies lifeless. Flesh, human and animal alike, litter the landscape. The sky is blackened, void of the sun, moon, or stars.

I press on, holding a mysterious object in my arms. I dare not look at it. Its hair is smooth, but it neither speaks nor moves. My sole focus is survival, my thoughts and questions neatly tucked away as I seek only one thing: my Creator. My constant cry is *Save me, God!*

Strength rises within me. My shoulders square, my chest lifts, and my head steadies. My steps grow firm, unshaken by the earth's tremors. A light appears in the distance, faint but unwavering. I fix my gaze on it, determined to reach it. The spirit guiding me fills me with resilience.

When I finally open my eyes, I'm leaning against the wall of our home. My father is staring down at me.

"Are you okay?" he asks.

I grunt in response, using my hands to steady myself on the mat. The sun beats down on my skin, and I gather my things to retreat inside. I'm hungry, thirsty, and drenched in sweat. After drawing water from the well for a shower, I feel renewed—light on my feet and quick in my movements.

I tell myself: *Do not seek what is outside you. Look within.*

Revolution

The sun rises, the moon and the stars follow, and the cycle repeats endlessly. Under the warm sun, I walk along the roadside next to the fence of the girls' high school. The air feels different, and my friends are few. Each step feels heavy, like a burden I can't shed.

Suddenly, a sleek car screeches to a halt in front of me. Startled, I step back, glaring at the vehicle. A young man steps out, dressed sharply in a pressed shirt, tailored trousers, and polished brown shoes. His enthusiasm catches me off guard.

"Are you Genifere?" he asks.

"Yes," I reply hesitantly.

He continues with a wide grin, "Sir ... sent me to pick you up for the dance audition."

I climb into the car, fastening my seatbelt at his request. We head toward the city's agricultural college auditorium, where the whole city has gathered. How did I not know about this event? I wonder, amazed by the crowd's size.

As we arrive, murmurs ripple through the room. "She's here! She's here! We have no chance now," some whisper nervously, though others cheer my arrival. Faces I don't recognize surround me—young hopefuls from neighboring cities, all here to try their luck.

The young man helps me register before introducing me to the person who lent his car. The hall is packed with over two hundred people, all dressed impeccably, each radiating talent and determination. I wait for my name to be called, listening to the chatter around me.

When it finally happens, I step forward, my heart pounding. The DJ leans toward me, asking for my song selection. I name a piece that resonates deeply with me—its rhythm is as captivating as its story, recounting the heartbreak of a woman whose husband strayed.

The music begins, and I lose myself in the performance. The crowd erupts in cheers, and my uncle smiles proudly from the audience. By the end, I'm lifted into the air by neighborhood friends, celebrating my success.

Out of the hundreds of participants, only eight are selected. A casually dressed man gathers us, leading us toward a classroom. As we pass, I see disappointed competitors, some weeping, others looking crushed. Discouraged parents scold their children. Among the chaos, I tread carefully, avoiding any conflicts.

In the classroom, we meet our trainer, who turns out to be a friend of my father. Though his expertise lies in traditional dance, we quickly adapted, working tirelessly to create routines for the competition.

When the big day arrives, the entire city lines the streets to cheer us on. The venue buzzes with excitement—media crews, corporate sponsors, and spectators flood the area. Despite the grandeur, nerves eat at me.

Finally, we perform, pouring every ounce of energy into our routine. The results are announced hours later: we've qualified for the playoffs. Although we ultimately place third and are eliminated, the city celebrates. For the first time, we've made it to national television.

Days pass, and life resumes its usual rhythm until Roger visits unexpectedly. He brings news of auditions for a festival in France, reigniting my dreams. On audition day, as I approach the venue, my mind and body separate for a brief moment, filled with both joy and thrill. I recognize familiar faces from previous competitions, as well as some renowned gurus of show business, and I wonder whom to ask about the room where the actual audition is taking place. I wander a bit until I notice a door that opens and closes with the passing crowd. Should I knock, or what should I do? Finally, I reach out, touch the door handle, and, wow, I step into a room I have never seen before. All the stars of our country are here, gathered to support their fellow producer, writer, and director, Mr. Koli.

As I make my way down the stairs, I feel every eye on me, and I struggle to walk without stumbling. At the stage, where dancers in vibrant outfits perform aerobics while drummers beat the djembe with relentless energy, the rhythm awakens something deep inside me. I move my head unconsciously to the beat until a man standing before the entire cast beckons me to sit behind him. After about 45 minutes of preparation, he turns to me and asks, "May I help you?"

"Oh, that was yesterday," he replies, causing my face to fall and my shoulders to slump. Yet he quickly reassures me, "It's okay, I will let you audition." At that moment, I am allowed to choose the rhythm and beat that speak to me. Standing in the center of the huge, black stage, I prepare to showcase my dancing skills. I know almost all the rhythms from every region of the country, and I feel that the more passion I display, the better my chances.

"The callback list will be posted in the lobby tomorrow morning," he announces.

Today is callback day, and nerves mix with excitement as I worry about the result. While I'm hand-washing my clothes, a friend rushes to my house and shouts, "Genifere, you made it! You have a meeting tomorrow at the venue, your name is fifth on the list." My mom watches us with a puzzled expression, as if trying to understand this unexpected news.

I now find myself part of an assembly—a comedy musical group, or so I thought. Today I learned that after two months of grueling rehearsals, a selection process will begin. Our schedule is relentless: from 7:00 AM to noon, then 2:30 PM to 6:00 PM, and finally from 8:00 PM to 1:00 AM. The group is a mix of comedians, dancers, musicians, drummers, and singers, and while my peers see me as a finalist, deep inside I struggle with doubts. During breaks, many encourage me, telling me I'm the best, yet the echoes of my father's voice, and even the faint murmur of God's voice, swirl in my mind. Ever since I began this journey, it has felt as though I were living in a box, suffocating. People say I'm shy, but they have no idea how crowded my thoughts are; I choose instead to focus on God's voice.

During rehearsals, I feel grounded; afterward, I feel transformed, as if I am a completely different person. In the second audition, I made it through! Yet, before I can truly rejoice, I learn that one final audition awaits, and then the hustle begins again, with no respite, only a constant struggle.

The pressure overwhelms me, and I remind myself, "My feet are my pen, and the stage is my paper." I start praying for help. One night, I have a brief dream in which I stand at the edge of sand and concrete, watching Caucasians play tennis on the hard surface. I don't understand its meaning until I'm selected for the finals. How did I learn of it? My boss asked if I had a passport and mentioned that all the girls needed to have their hair braided. We had the entire day to get it done, and there I was, sitting on the main street, getting my hair braided, when Dad and his friend approached me.

"Genifere, your friend just told me that you're going to Paris tonight," Dad says. "Which friend?" I reply. "The short one with big eyes," he responds. "Me? Going to Paris? Not a chance!" I retort. Then Dad looks at his friend and says, "I told you the boy lies. Who would take her to Paris? Come on, let's go." As they walk away, I glance back and murmur, "So, you don't see everything?"

At the airport, an unknown voice echoes in my mind, "They will send you home because you are a mistake." Louder than God's voice, it haunts me as I take my seat on the airplane, head lowered. We soar through the clouds, and that same voice insists that once we land in Paris, I'll be sent back. I break away from the group during passport checks until finally, when we report to our hotel, I find a measure of relief. As Mom always says, her God will help me if I call out to Him, well, here I am in Paris!

The Light Within

The room is quiet except for the soft rustle of the wind outside. I sit by the window, gazing at the vast expanse of the horizon, where the sun dips low and paints the sky with hues of amber and violet. It's the same sky I've looked up at countless times, but today it feels different. There's a strange sense of finality as if the universe is whispering, *This is the moment you've been waiting for.*

I've danced in the shadows of my past, stumbled in the dark of self-doubt, and burned under the intensity of a world that labeled me a "witch." But I've also soared through dreams that terrified and healed me through moments of pure brilliance that lifted me beyond earthly bounds.

As a child, my red hair flamed with my every mood, reflecting the tempest within me. Now, it shines with quiet strength, no longer dictated by chaos but by an unshakable sense of purpose.

For years, I searched for validation in the eyes of others in the applause of strangers, the smiles of my parents, and the fleeting praise of mentors. But I've come to understand a truth that no performance, no competition, and no worldly success can teach you. The light I chased wasn't out there, it was always within.

I think back to that day, leaning against the wall of our home, drenched in sweat and trembling from an otherworldly experience. I had looked within and found not answers, but courage. Courage to step into a world that didn't understand me. Courage to use my "gifts" not as a burden, but as a guide.

In the end, the visions, the surreal dreams that lifted me to impossible heights and plunged me into unimaginable depths, weren't about predicting my future or glorifying my destiny. They were mirrors, reflecting the raw potential and untapped strength I carried all along.

Today, as I prepare for my next journey, this time to a stage in Paris, where the world will watch, I feel no fear. The applause will come and go, the spotlight will fade, and the curtains will fall. But the fire within me will remain, an eternal flame that no shadow can extinguish.

As I stand to leave, I catch my reflection in the glass. My hair catches the dying sunlight, flickering shades of copper and gold. I no longer see the girl who feared being different, who fought against the tide of judgment and rejection. I see a woman who embraced the unknown, trusted her spirit, and discovered the light within.

With a steady breath, I open the door and step outside. The world feels vast and alive, every sound and color sharper than before. My spirit soars, untethered, as I walk toward my future, not as a dancer, a dreamer, or a survivor, but as myself.

The light that guides me isn't in the sky or in the praise of others. It's in me, and it always has been.